PROCESS IMPROVEMENT
A HANDBOOK FOR MANAGERS

For David

PROCESS IMPROVEMENT

A handbook for managers

Sarah Cook

Gower

Published by
Gower Publishing Limited
Gower House
Croft Road
Aldershot
Hampshire GU11 3HR
England

Gower
Old Post Road
Brookfield
Vermont 05036
USA

British Library Cataloguing in Publication Data
Cook, Sarah
  Process Improvement: Handbook for Managers
  I. Title
  658.562

ISBN 0–566–07633–0

Library of Congress Cataloging-in-Publication Data

Cook, Sarah.
  Process improvement: a handbook for managers/Sarah Cook.
    p.   cm.
  Includes bibliographical references and index.
  ISBN 0–566–07633–0 (hardback)
  1. Reengineering (Management)   I. Title.
HD58.87.C66 1995
658.4'069—dc20   95–30773
                                                              CIP

Typeset in Century by Bournemouth Colour Press, Parkstone, Dorset and printed in Great Britain by Biddles Ltd, Guildford

CONTENTS

1 Process Improvement in Perspective

Gives definitions of: a process; process thinking; process improvement; process redesign; business process reengineering. Shows that process thinking is a tool for bringing about organizational change and examines the need for such change. Outlines the implications of organizational change and the skills required for successful organizational change management, giving as an example how First Direct handled the cultural issues surrounding process improvement.

2 The Beginnings

Looks at total quality management and customer care as areas in which process redesign plays an important part. Shows that process thinking can be a mechanism for empowering employees and how benchmarking has brought awareness of the need for business process improvement. Describes the roles of Hammer and Champy in promoting the technique as a tool for effective organizational change.

3 Benefits and Problems

Discusses, with examples, the benefits of business process improvement and outlines potential problems and pitfalls. Describes seven steps to overcome them and ensure the successful implementation of process improvements.

LIST OF FIGURES

PREFACE

'Business Reengineering does not sound revolutionary, but it is,' states Charles Handy.

'Reengineering is new and it has to be done,' says Peter Drucker.

'I haven't seen a company yet that wouldn't benefit from some sort of Reengineering' – James Champy.

Management consultants such as these, along with senior management in many organizations across the globe, believe strongly in the power of business process improvement. Many businesses who have introduced process improvement in their companies demonstrate through their results that business reengineering has brought quantum leaps in performance and profitability.

But the warning signs are there too. As one recent survey reports 'It's not for everyone, and sometimes it fails to deliver'.

This book sets out to dispel the myths surrounding the topic. It will help the reader to:

– recognize the benefits of business process improvement, the problems and the pitfalls. Recognize also how to link process improvement efforts to organizational goals;
– understand the terminology surrounding the topic and obtain an overview of the stages of process improvement;
– gain a greater understanding of the background and origins of process improvement;
– identify processes in need of improvement, undertake an assessment and detailed analysis of redesign and implement effective solutions;
– create a system for monitoring and reviewing improvement activities.

The book, therefore, is designed to act as a practical guide to business process improvement. It provides a framework which managers, team leaders, quality co-ordinators, consultants and trainers can use to bring about incremental or step change within an organization.

This book can be used as a guide to improve current processes in a discrete area of an organization or as a means of totally rethinking the way a company goes about doing business.

The opening chapters provide background information on the origins of process improvement and how it can be used as a change management tool.

The author outlines a four-step approach to process improvement. Each stage provides you with in-depth knowledge of problem-solving techniques and how to apply these within an organizational context.

Each chapter concludes with an overview of the tools contained in the chapter. These are also reprised in the summary chapter, Process Improvement in Action, which contains examples of process redesign in action. The final section of the book gives a useful library of sources and resources on process improvement.

Sarah Cook

CHAPTER

1

PROCESS IMPROVEMENT IN PERSPECTIVE

The 1990s have seen continuous and rapid change in the way businesses operate. Increasing globalization, greater competition, the growing power of customers, mean that organizations have to constantly reappraise the way they conduct business in order to add value to their customers and to maintain their competitive advantage.

In response to the demands of the marketplace, many organizations have recognized the need to change the way they operate. Improving, reorganizing or reinventing the processes by which a business achieves its customer satisfaction is a powerful mechanism for change.

Over the past five years organizations as different as DHL, Rank Xerox, ICL, National & Provincial, Microsoft and Ford have benefited from improving their internal processes. Some have achieved this under the banner of 'business process reengineering', others through continuous improvement programmes, best practice initiatives or process redesign.

To many managers the term 'business process re-engineering' may seem a 1990s vogue, just as 'management by objectives' was in the 1970s and 'total quality management' in the 1990s.

Others may be confused by the plethora of terms surrounding the topic – core process redesign, business process redesign, process reengineering, network redesign, process innovation, network reengineering, process management. In order to avoid confusion, here is a definition of each of the terms associated with the word 'process' used in a business context.

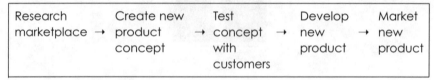

Figure 1.1 Example of the process of new product development in its simplest form

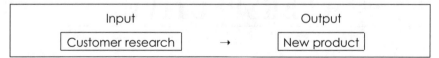

Figure 1.2 Example of the input and output of the new product development process

 ## What is a process?

A process is a series of steps or sequence of business activities the outcome of which is to achieve customer satisfaction by providing the customer with what they need, when they require it and in the manner which they expect. For a company to successfully create and market a new product to meet customer demands, for example, a number of activities have to be undertaken (see Figure 1.1). A process, therefore, always has an input and an output (see Figure 1.2). The stages between input and output involve differing variables, such as the quality of activities involved, how they are organized, timescales and composition, cost, people resources, degree of difficulty, accuracy, speed and flexibility.

 ## What is process thinking?

Process thinking involves reviewing the variables in a process in order to improve its efficiency and effectiveness.

Process thinking is the generic term applied to improving an organization's current performance by rethinking the way its business activities are organized. This often involves rethinking the way a company produces its work so that the customer receives a better service. This means ensuring that the activities are undertaken for the customer's benefit, not for the ease of managing the organization.

In the health service, for example, improvements are being undertaken in the primary care sector to offer the customer a better service. In some areas pilot schemes are being conducted where people in the community who require advisory services, be it medical, to do with social services or general benefits, can obtain advice and consultation through one central point rather than contacting separate offices, such as individual doctors' practices, dentists, benefits agency, housing officer, etc.

This is an illustration of process thinking as senior managers in the areas piloting the schemes have recognized that their customers often have a series of interwoven and interrelated issues/concerns which need to be addressed and which can be fulfilled through one centre or process rather than separate, different processes.

 ## What is process improvement?

Process improvement is a method of improving the way a discrete set of business activities is organized and managed. This often involves making improvements to current systems.

An example of process improvement is the improvements which one large organization made to the way it conducted its training and development cycle. It had a well-defined process for analysing training needs and designing and delivery training programmes. It evaluated the effectiveness of the training at the end of each course, but it did not obtain feedback on how well the training was being put into practice. The process was improved, therefore, by carrying out post-training evaluations in the workplace.

 ## What is process redesign?

Process redesign is a method of developing a new process or

significantly altering a current one to better meet the needs of customers. Process redesign is usually more comprehensive than process improvement as it involves understanding customer requirements and developing processes which best match customer needs. The new processes which are created may be significantly different from existing ones.

An example of process redesign is the method adopted by many banks and building societies to deal with mortgage applications. Rather than local branches handling each application the process has often been simplified via the introduction of a centralized mortgage application unit serving a cluster of branches, thereby shortening the length of time required to process each application.

 ## What is business process reengineering?

Business process reengineering is a method of bringing about dramatic change in the way a business does business. It usually involves starting with 'a clean sheet of paper' to determine how key business activities need to be reconfigured to meet customer demands. This often involves restructuring the business in parts or in whole or recreating a new one.

First Direct is an example of a business which, by offering its customers a 24-hour service by telephone, has completely transformed the way banking services are made available to customers.

 ## Process thinking as a tool for change

Whatever approach is adopted by an organization, be it process improvement, process redesign or business process reengineering, process thinking should be viewed as one of the techniques in a toolbox designed to bring about organizational change.

One organization recently undertook a large-scale review of its business processes. The outcome was a radical restructure in the

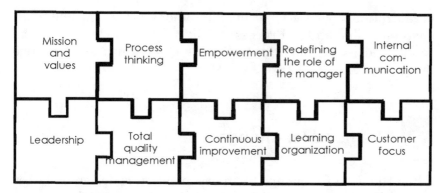

Figure 1.3 Example of the jigsaw of techniques for organizational change

way it operated both in terms of its order to delivery cycle and its new product development process. This involved changing many parts of its business operations to achieve greater customer satisfaction and retention. Yet the review and subsequent implementation were not carried out under a 'process redesign' banner. Senior managers believed strongly that the terminology would immediately raise barriers amongst its workforce who were resistant to what it saw as 'American hype'. This was particularly so because many misconceptions exist about process redesign and business process reengineering in terms of their meaning and use. In addition, the management of the organization viewed process thinking and the techniques of process redesign and business process reengineering as one element of an interlocking jigsaw of tools and techniques for bringing about organizational change (see Figure 1.3).

The company's approach is in line with that of many organizations who introduce new ways of working but not under the reengineering banner. Indeed, a study undertaken by COBRA[1] (Consultants and Opportunities in Business Restructuring – an Analysis) into 100 European companies confirm that reengineering has become associated with negative aspects of downsizing and cost reduction. It is not always seen as a positive force for change.

The author's view, which is shared by many practitioners and management consultants who specialize in business process improvement, is that process thinking should be seen as one of a set of drivers towards achieving organizational goals. It is a positive force which helps speed up change and can bring an organization's strategy, leadership and culture in line with customer demands. Process thinking therefore should be recognized as an important element of organizational change programmes.

 ## The need for change

Often the need for change in an organization is driven by forces external to the company. Factors in the environment, classified as STEP factors – sociological, technological, economic and political forces – can affect business performance. Take, for example, the hypothetical case of a company operating in the pharmaceutical market.

Organizational change may have been driven by a number of external factors, among them:

Sociological factors
1.   Move towards healthier lifestyle.
2.   Greater awareness of health issues.
3.   Ageing population.

Technological factors
1.   Advances in information technology.
2.   Improvements in manufacturing processes.
3.   Medical advances.

Economic factors
1.   Recessionary economic climate.
2.   Increased cost awareness among customer base.
3.   High cost of raw materials.

Political factors
1.   Legislation governing sale of drugs over the counter.
2.   Changes in the Health Service.
3.   European Union regulations.

These STEP factors may be catalysts for change just as factors governing the near environment may necessitate change.

Professor Michael Porter of Harvard Business School has developed a useful framework for analysing market forces (Figure 1.4). In addition to identifying the power of customers,

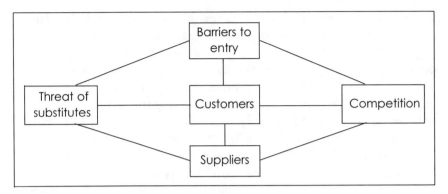

Figure 1.4 Porter's five forces

competition and suppliers, his framework pinpoints the threats posed by substitute products or services to an organization's market position and how the ease of entry to the marketplace determines competitive advantage.

Customers

Changes in customer base, changes in customer demand, changes in customer expectations lead to the need for organizations to realign their products and services to meet customer expectations.

Airline customers are a good example. Increases in foreign travel and higher expectations of the quality of service have meant that airlines continuously have had to make improvement in their service to meet the demands of the customers.

Customers, it appears, are becoming more demanding. There is greater awareness of customer rights. Customers are no longer satisfied with second-class service. Statistics show that complaints are on the increase. To stay ahead, organizations have to change their behaviour and attitude towards the customer.

Competition

As marketplaces are becoming increasingly crowded and competition heightens, it is increasingly harder for organizations to gain market share. Indeed, it has been established that there exists only a short-term 'strategic window' in which an organization can maximize its competitive advantage before competitors match and exceed its position, thereby robbing it of sales. Amstrad, who were innovators in the field of personal computers, are an example of an organization who won competitive advantage only to lose it to the plethora of competition who also entered the market.

The focus of the 1990s has become to attract and *retain* existing customers. There can be few businesses whose organizational mission is not to satisfy its customer requirements. In the face of competitors whose mission is all too probably to also satisfy customer needs, businesses have to be prepared to change if they are to survive.

Suppliers

The 1990s have seen a minor revolution in the relationship organizations have with their suppliers. 'Partnership sourcing' and 'just in time' principles have led to a decrease in the quantity of suppliers many organizations deal with. In turn this has brought about higher expectations of the quality of the relationship and the service levels provided by suppliers.

Barriers to entry

Changes in marketplaces can also be effected when barriers to entry are low. Who would have thought, for example, that traditional high street banks and building societies would be threatened by the entry into the marketplace of companies like Marks & Spencer Financial Services who offer personal loans and financial services in the same way as their traditional rivals?

Threat of substitutes

A further threat and driver for change is created when substitute products or services become available. Betamax videos are an example of a product which, although arguably superior to its rival VHS, has seen its marketplace diminish in the UK through substitution by consumers of its product for VHS versions.

The speed of change

The challenge facing many organizations, therefore, is to keep ahead of changes in the far and near environment, thereby progressing and growing as a business. Merely to keep pace with changes in the environment leads to a steady but non-progressive state. To fall behind the rate of change in the environment means the company will be overtaken by its competitors.

Organizations can deal with change in two ways. They can adopt the route of:

– incremental change – when improvements are made on a gradual and sometimes imperceptible basis;

or

– step change – which involves large-scale and drastic differences in the way the organization goes about its business.

An example of incremental change in an organization such as a delivery company would be the introduction of improved technology over time, improvements in training and development of employees, increases in the number of delivery vehicles available, etc.

If the same delivery company were to undertake step change this might involve their setting up a completely new form of service centre where delivery drivers act as salespeople and delivery is effected in a more speedy and reliable manner than by the competition.

There are advantages and disadvantages to each of the forms that change can take.

Incremental change

Advantages
❏ Change is progressive
❏ Less threatening to people involved

❑ Builds on current strengths
❑ Tactical
❑ Less disruptive to organization

Disadvantages

○ Keeps existing paradigms
○ May not address in-built weaknesses
○ Takes longer to achieve
○ Potential gain smaller
○ Less strategic

Step Change

Advantages

❑ Breaks paradigms
❑ Enforces new methods of working and new ways of thinking
❑ Can bring organizations closer to the customer
❑ Swift to achieve
❑ Identifies root causes of problems

Disadvantages

○ Impact on organizational structure is greater
○ Affect on people can be dramatic
○ Needs strong leadership
○ Requires effective change management

 Change and process thinking

'Process thinking' provides management with a tool which can bring about either step or incremental change.

Process improvement, which has been used as a technique for change since the 1980s, produces valuable changes. However, some circumstances, brought about by volatile external and internal factors, require organizations to cause immediate and dramatic improvements in areas which are of strategic

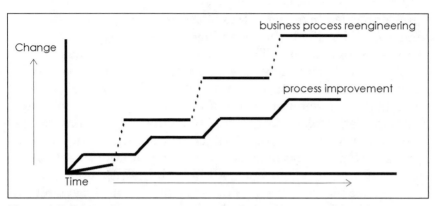

Figure 1.5 Process improvement versus business process reengineering

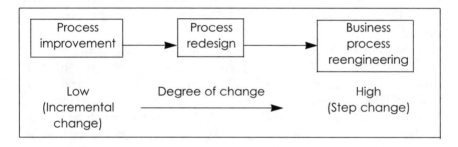

Figure 1.6 Process thinking and degree of change

importance to the business. Here business process reengineering, which brings about step change, is called for. See Figure 1.5.

The Japanese have been working since 1945 to bring about continuous process improvement. They have not needed to make step change as they are typically more productive than their Western counterparts. Although many British industries have undertaken programmes to improve processes, there was until the 1990s a reluctance among many managers to address some of the root problems facing their businesses. Introducing new product lines or opening new markets held more appeal than concentrating on streamlining existing operations and making them more customer friendly and cost effective.

US and European organizations such as Ford have used both process improvement and business process reengineering to bring about various degrees of change (see Figure 1.6). In the mid-1980s the success of process improvement projects which helped rationalize Ford's central accounting accounts payable, for example, led to a recognition of the power of process thinking. Managers identified the need for a structured approach to process reengineering. There was a call for language to be developed and training and support to be provided to process improvement teams. In the late 1980s and early 1990s special workshops and seminars were developed in order to roll out a common methodology for process reengineering. To date nearly 5,000 team leaders have attended the training and process reengineering has become part of a way of working towards continuous improvement for Ford in both the US and Europe.

The success of Ford's approach has been dependent on employee involvement in the development and implementation of the current methodology. What many organizations who undertake process redesign initiatives forget is that processes are operated by people.

This book sets out an approach to business process improvement which can be applied across a variety of different businesses and industries. What will make or break the successful application of the implementation of process thinking, however, will be the way in which the people involved in the leadership and implementation of the project interact with other people affected by the changes to be brought about by process thinking.

One British food manufacturer, for example, undertook a process redesign exercise. As a result , it introduced a new way of working among its employees to encourage greater focus on the customer. The concept was to develop cross-functional, multi-disciplined teams throughout the organization. Traditional management titles were abolished in favour of a 'team leader' badge. Employees were empowered to take responsibility for decisions affecting their area of work. Traditional reporting structures were abolished.

The initial result was confusion. Employees felt that the new team structure had been imposed on them. They were wary of their team leaders whom they still deferred to as managers. Many were reluctant to take responsibility for decisions. The leadership and commitment to the new way of working was considered by employees as being very weak. Criticism was voiced of the way the new structure had been introduced as it was felt that there had been unnecessary redundancies and the reasons for changing the status quo were unclear. What began as an exercise in business process improvement with a sound rationale very quickly turned into a communications fiasco with many wounded parties.

Successful business process improvement, therefore, has to be viewed as an interactive and participative process. It requires all the skills of successful change management:

– Careful preparation.
– Strong leadership and commitment to change.
– Thinking through the likely problems as well as the benefits in terms of customers, employees and business implications.
– A plan of action with clear objectives and measurements.
– Information, encouragement and support for those involved so they 'buy in' to the new process.
– Expectations that change will take time.

 ## People's reaction to change

In any business process improvement project, therefore, careful attention should be paid to minimizing people's resistance to change.

Many people go through different reactions to changes not only in the workplace but also in their personal lives (see Figure 1.7).

The initial reaction of most people when they are faced with a change at work in which they have had no say is a feeling of shock, powerlessness and/or anger and hurt. This is often followed by a period of denial when people concentrate on the past and focus their energies on conserving the status quo. Where people perceive the proposed changes as a threat rather than an opportunity they often show their resistance through their behaviour at work – withdrawal from the team, grumblings and negative views being aired or lack of co-operation are typical of this phase.

Unless the negative aspects of people's reaction to change are managed successfully there will be low commitment to the new process. Organizations who have successfully implemented business process improvement have focused their employees on the future, they have helped them explore the possibilities of the

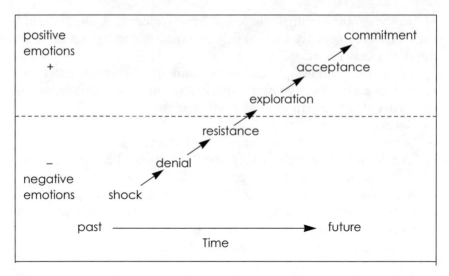

Figure 1.7 People's reaction to change

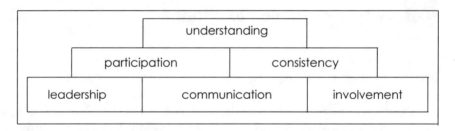

Figure 1.8 Building-blocks required for successful business process improvement

new process and accept that the change will benefit both employees and the organization.

How is the transition from denial and resistance to acceptance and commitment achieved? There are six building-blocks in the successful management of change.

Leadership

Strong and visible commitment by the leaders of an organization to business process improvement and the changes it will bring – both in words and actions; for example, the amount of time given by senior management to the project, the degree of contact they have with those involved, speak more than words.

Communication

Informing employees about the initiative, what it entails, why it is happening, what will happen, when it will take place, what the likely results will be, who will be affected, what is the programme, what have been the successes and learning points.

Involvement

Consulting people who will be involved in the changes: customers, suppliers, employees and other stakeholders. Involving them in the process of redesigning improvements, seeking and listening to and acting on their views.

Participation

Encouraging teamwork and ownership among employees. Recognizing that it takes the commitment of every one of the team to make the new process work effectively. Sharing common aims and values.

Consistency

Making certain that the same message is reinforced when the going gets tough as well as when times are good. Communicating the need for change and its benefits time after time. Making certain that desired and actual behaviours are consistent.

Understanding

Understanding that change can be difficult. Showing empathy and patience with those that find it difficult while at the same time generating understanding of the benefits of change.

The cultural implications of change

Businesses who have successfully implemented process improvements, therefore, have recognized that in addressing

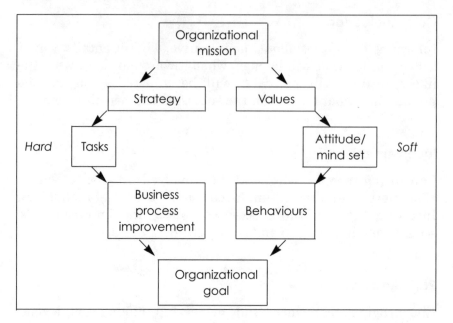

Figure 1.9 Hard versus soft approaches to change

processes, they need to also consider the impact the changes will make on an organization's culture – its way of working, its values and beliefs, 'the way we do business around here'.

Herein lies a difficulty: processes are tangible, they can be readily observed and mapped out. They have a discernible outcome. Culture is intangible. It is underpinned by the values of people which in turn make up the 'mind sets' or paradigms which are exemplified in the behaviour of the employees of an organization. Yet, to the customer, a business's culture is evident just as there is evidence in the marketplace of an organization's presence, through its products and services, how it is promoted, its pricing structure and its physical accessibility or location.

The failure of many techniques used in change management such as process thinking is that they concentrate on the 'hard' aspects of organizational change rather than the soft (see Figure 1.9).

As we will see in the later chapters, it is how the cultural aspects of a business process improvement programme are managed that determine to a great extent its success.

An example of step change

One organization who has dealt with both the hard and softer cultural issues surrounding process improvement is First Direct. First Direct has rewritten the rules of banking by offering its customers a 24-hour banking service by telephone. First Direct is acknowledged as the market leader in the UK for direct banking and financial service. Launched in October 1989, First Direct is the only organization in the UK that provides a full person-to-person banking service, over the telephone, 24 hours a day, 365 days a year.

Customers can call one of First Direct's banking representatives at any time of the day or night to conduct an extensive set of financial transactions, from a simple balance update to organizing a personal loan or mortgage.

First Direct grew out of the conviction of its parent company, Midland Bank, that the time was right for a complete change in direction in personal banking. Midland wanted to grow its market share among upscale customers, something it was unable to do by acquisition and which was extremely difficult to do by organic growth. The industry was oversupplied; profits were hard to achieve; cost cutting was a central feature across all banks as they increasingly found themselves competing with the lower cost base of the building societies; and customers were becoming more discerning – even hostile – demanding far higher levels of customer service and a return to a more personal approach from their banks.

Radical thinking was required by Midland to break free from these constraints and a development team – called Project Raincloud – was charged with this task. The team knew there was a place in the market for a totally different kind of banking service. What they did not know at that time was how it should be different.

For some time Midland had been collecting evidence that there was a growing number of customers with a deep-rooted frustration with the traditional banking system. This was confirmed by MORI research commissioned by First Direct just before its launch which revealed that customers were progressively making less use of the branch network. According to MORI, one in five people had not visited their branch in the last month, 51 per cent said they would rather visit their branch as little as possible and 48 per cent had never met their bank manager. Encouragingly, 27 per cent wished there were more things they could get their bank to do for them by telephone.

This research was echoed by the Henley Centre for Forecasting whose studies found that consumer demand for better service was higher among banks than for any other retail sector. Their research revealed that friendly and knowledgeable staff were considered most important alongside convenient opening hours and quick and easy transactions.

The way seemed to be pointing to some form of direct banking – dealing with customers over the telephone. But the research emphasized that there had to be human contact. According to MORI, three-quarters of those interested in a telephone banking service wanted a person on the other end of the line – not a computer.

In search of more answers, the Project Raincloud team surveyed the banking market across the world – in Europe, North America and Australia. The trawl revealed that a tremendous number of financial transactions were being carried out by telephone, although most companies offered only embryonic teleservicing – extensions of the branch network.

To provide customers with the kind of service Midland believed they now required meant starting from scratch. None of the traditional banking models could be adapted.

From the outset First Direct has tried to create an ethos where all staff really value their relationship with the customer, in direct contrast to the more traditional 'It's more than my job's worth' mentality. To foster this, managers are encouraged to develop the roles of leadership and guidance, not interference and instruction.

A key attraction for customers is First Direct's ease of access and approachability and this has to be reflected across the entire culture of the organization, with little hierarchy and much democracy. One way of avoiding an 'upstairs downstairs' mentality, for instance, is by using first names among employees, whether banking representative or chief executive. This is a culture unique in British banking, where it is still common for staff to refer to superiors as Mr, Mrs or Miss, where managers are usually segregated from their staff by separate offices on separate floors, and where staff are expected to approach management only through the person directly above them in the hierarchy.

This approach is combined with a completely open-plan working environment. First Direct's operations centre is located in Leeds, where all the banking representatives and financial advisers are based. This comprises 70,000 square feet of single-storey open-plan office, with an additional 30,000 square feet situated within the same building, but there are no closed offices and no doors to close.

 ## Summary

- A process is a series of business activities whose outcome is to achieve customer satisfaction.
- Process thinking is the generic term applied to rethinking the way an organization orders its business activities.
- Process improvement involves making improvements to current systems, whereas process redesign is a method of developing a new process or significantly altering a current one.
- Business process reengineering is a means of bringing about step change by 'starting with a clean sheet of paper' and reconfiguring the process to meet customer demands.
- Process thinking is one of the techniques in a toolbox designed to bring about organizational change.
- Factors in both the far and the near environment can act as catalysts for change.
- Business improvements can be made either on an incremental basis or as step change.
- Successful business process improvement has to be viewed as an interactive and participative process requiring skills in change management.
- In particular practitioners adopting process thinking as a tool for change should be mindful of the cultural implications of change.

CHAPTER

2

THE BEGINNINGS

In order to better understand what is business process improvement and how best to use the technique, it is helpful to be aware of its background and origins. As we saw in Chapter 1, business process improvement is one element of a jigsaw of tools and techniques for bringing about organizational change (see Figure 2.1). It should be viewed as complementary to other initiatives, and indeed as being capable of running alongside many such initiatives, as change projects are interactive.

 ## Total quality management and customer care

Many organizations have adopted a total quality management approach to satisfying customer requirements (see Figure 2.2). Others have begun programmes to instil a customer focus throughout their companies. Some organizations run both initiatives in parallel as well as initiating quality systems through the adoption of ISO 9000 quality standards. These programmes are designed to create changes in the culture of organizations, to make them less bureaucratic, more customer focused and productive.

Both total quality management (TQM) and customer care programmes aim to bring about changes in employees' attitudes, behaviours and skills. One of the difficulties in the past that has been encountered in bringing about these changes, however, is that often the organizational context in which the employees are expected to work is not changed. Hence, the way an organization

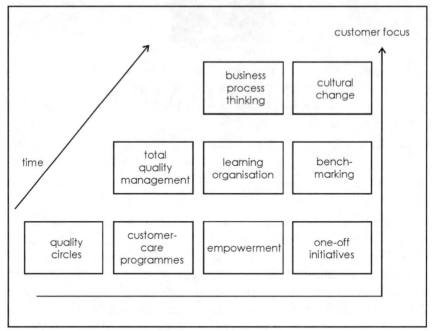

Figure 2.1 Techniques for creating a customer focus

Traditional organization		Customer-focused organization
Needs of the organization	v.	Needs of the customer
Hierarchical structure	v.	Flattened structure
Rules and regulations	v.	Initiative and empowerment
Management decisions	v.	Team decisions

Figure 2.2 Traditional versus customer-focused organization

goes about doing business may impede its effectiveness in satisfying the customer, irrespective of how well it manages to succeed in changing employees' attitudes and behaviours to be more customer focused.

Take as an example a customer who wishes to have connected the supply of electricity in a new office building they are about to take over. They telephone the electricity board to make arrangements. The telephonist tells them they must visit an electricity showroom in person to arrange for an appointment. When they visit the showroom they are told they need to send for

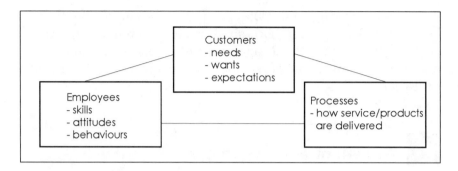

Figure 2.3 Three factors affecting performance

an application form which has to be processed by the central office. Once the customer receives notification that the application has been accepted they need to revisit the showroom to pay for the connection. They must then telephone the central office to make an appointment. At this stage and seven days later the customer becomes very agitated! Employees' customer handling skills in this example, therefore, will only succeed in placating an angry customer rather than eliminating the source of complaint as the organization's systems and procedures are long-winded and unfriendly to the customer.

Often, because TQM and customer care programmes focus on cultural attitudes, they do not improve what is happening to the customer. There may well be improvement in the short term but staff can become cynical when nothing really changes for the better. Many organizations who undertake TQM and customer care programmes recognize, therefore, that process redesign should become part of the continuous improvement activity. They see processes, just like people and customers, as being three key factors that affect performance (Figure 2.3).

When Nationwide Building Society, for example, undertook a customer care programme designed to attract and retain greater numbers of customers, it obtained feedback from both its external and internal customers which indicated that the efficiency of many of its processes could be improved. Part of its change programme, therefore, focused on the length of time it took to undertake many of its core processes, such as mortgage applications. The results were improvements in both efficiency and customer satisfaction.

Process thinking and TQM are therefore complementary to each other. In fact they both share some common assumptions, such as the need for the development of an organizational vision and the commitment of senior management to the change process.

 ## Growth of empowerment

Companies who wish to become closer to their customers recognize that responsibilities for decisions affecting the customer must be given to those people who have greatest contact with the customer – usually front line staff! Linked to many customer care and TQM initiatives, therefore, is the desire to 'empower' employees. This is not only in terms of how they deal with customers but also how they take responsibility for their own training and development (hence the 'learning organization').

There has been a growing trend to create self-managing teams in many organizations. These teams are usually formed from people working in the same area who provide support to each other. UK restaurant chain Harvester Restaurants, for example, has created self-managing teams in many of its restaurant outlets. The teams are responsible for running the outlet, recruitment, selection and training of staff, serving customers and liaison with head office. The result has been a higher level of employee motivation and greater customer satisfaction and retention.

The team approach means that employees can respond faster to customer needs. It calls for the breaking down of many traditional structures. Reorganizing the workforce in natural groupings based around a product, service or vertical market, rather than a functional department, means that organizational structures and processes need to adapt to the trend.

Process improvement has been used, therefore, as a means of rethinking the way the organization operates. Process thinking is a mechanism used to empower employees by transforming organizational structures from pyramid to T shapes (see Figure 2.4).

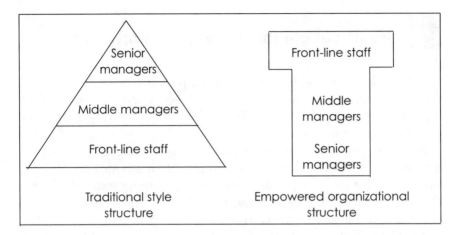

Figure 2.4 Traditional-style versus empowered-style organizational structure

National & Provincial Building Society set out in the late 1980s to create an environment which was truly customer focused. It abandoned the traditional hierarchical structure typical of many building societies and banks and formed a series of teams throughout the organization, who in turn reported to other teams including a team of senior managers. The Society used techniques such as business process improvement to rationalize its operations.

Jeans maker Levi has developed a strategy to influx a new spirit into the workplace which has improved its profit performance and the morale of its employees. Throughout its history, Levi's operators knew nothing but the piecework pay system. The more work you did, the more money you made above basic pay. By the late 1980s there was a growing realization that there must be better ways to organize the workplace to avoid the high costs and mistakes involved in the manufacturing process. In one plant employees were asked to design a new approach. They organized themselves round teams responsible for shepherding jeans from cutting through all the sewing steps to shipping. They set themselves their own production goals over a minimum set by plant management. They used process thinking on the production line to improve efficiency. This empowered approach has been copied by other plants. The result is a manufacturing time of one day as opposed to six under the old system, a higher degree of productivity, competitiveness and staff morale.

Use of benchmarking and best practice

Benchmarking is a technique which helps organizations measure their effectiveness and efficiency in comparison with other organizations. It is a technique which has been growing in popularity over the past ten years.

Xerox were among the first companies to use benchmarking on a widespread basis to help create competitive advantage. During the 1970s the company was leader in the copying market. Yet by the 1980s its market share had become eroded by the influx of cheaper competitors. Xerox recognized that it had to fight for survival. So it studied companies who were considered to be 'best in class' in each of the processes in place within its organization. It established what was perceived to be best practice as its benchmark and reorganized the way it ran its operation in line with this standard. This management technique helped Xerox identify gaps in performance. It highlighted differences in organizational processes and set new standards of performance.

Benchmarking would not have been successful, however, for Xerox and other companies, unless they understood their own processes before looking at 'best in class'.

Benchmarking is now an established technique for bringing about improvements in performance. Surveys indicate that up to 70 per cent of UK companies have adopted the tool, and benchmarking consultancies have sprung up to facilitate the process. The use of benchmarking as a management tool has brought with it, therefore, an awareness of the need for business process improvement.

Hammer, Champy and business process reengineering

As we have seen, a number of trends emerged in the later 1980s and early 1990s which led organizations to focus on business processes. These can be summed up as:
-   The need to create a customer focus.
-   Adoption of total quality management, quality systems and

customer care initiatives.
– Growth of empowerment and adoption of the concept of the 'learning' organization.
– Adoption of benchmarking and best practice techniques.
These trends have arisen in a recessionary economic climate where the need for greater efficiency has produced mass downsizing and restructuring, scarce resources and limited budgets and increased use of technology to increase output.

In 1983 the Massachusetts Institute of Technology (MIT) conducted a research study into the likely impact of information technology in the 1990s. Its findings identified the importance of business processes in contributing to the success of organization.

During the 1980s companies such as Ford used process thinking tools to reduce its workforce in the accounts payable department from 400 to 100 and Bell Atlantic to cut its delivery times from 15 days to just one.

In early 1993 Michael Hammer and James Champy, two American business consultants, launched the fashion for 'business process reengineering' based on their experiences of business process reengineering with US companies. Their book, *Reengineering the corporation: a manifesto for business revolution*, became a bestseller in both the US and the UK. Hammer and Champy argue that organizations have to confront the reality that old ways of doing business do not work any more. The book's central theme is that in today's increasingly changing environment companies need to organize themselves to work around processes rather than tasks.

Hammer defines the techniques as: 'The fundamental rethinking and radical redesign of business processes to achieve dramatic improvements in critical contemporary measures of performance such as cost, quality, service and speed.' In an interview in the *Financial Times* on 5 February 1995, James Champy sets out his view of reengineering:

> The big idea about reengineering is that it assumes we need to redesign work starting with a clean sheet of paper. It is particularly about redesigning processes, how we develop new products. What it attracts is the fragmentation of work and the bureaucratic structures which we have built in our large organizations and government agencies.

The authors argue that three forces – customers, competition and change – challenge the way organizations do business. They question 'Why do we do what we do at all?' Successful reengineering involves looking at entire processes that cut across organizational boundaries, breaking with tradition and using information technology in a creative way. By adopting this technique the book promises that dramatic improvements will be achieved in customer service, through improvements in time cycles, reduction in cost and improvements in quality.

The book can be criticized on two fronts. First, the examples are drawn from the US and there are few illustrations of where business process reengineering has been applied in Europe. Second, there are few pages devoted to the crucial element of the people factor involved in business reengineering.

Champy admits, 'I don't think we appreciated the degree to which management would have to change in order to be successful at reengineering'.[2] In Champy's further book, *Reengineering Management – a mandate for new leadership* he argues that you cannot change the nature of the work without changing what managerial work is. He sees managerial work as needing a far greater external focus. The book advocates a greater awareness of the cultural questions surrounding change.

Since Hammer and Champy's widely published writings and talks on the topic business process reengineering has become an established concept, such as quality or TQM in the 1980s. Problems have occurred where it has also been adopted as a panacea by some organizations, many of whom have spectacularly failed in their endeavours to transform their organizations.

In the next chapter we discuss the benefits and pitfalls of business process improvements in more depth.

 Summary

- This chapter provides an outline of the emergence of process thinking in the late 1980s and early 1990s.
- It demonstrates the links between process thinking, TQM and customer care.
- It shows how the growth of empowerment and 'learning organizations' has been facilitated by process thinking.

- It outlines how a detailed understanding is needed of processes in order to instigate benchmarking and best practice studies.
- Finally, it discusses the role that Hammer and Champy have played in championing the technique as a tool for effective organizational change.

CHAPTER

3

BENEFITS AND PROBLEMS

In October 1994 the front pages of many British newspapers proclaimed that it takes 20 civil servants in the Department of Health to answer one letter from the public. A reply must go through 72 stages of red tape before it can be signed, sealed and sent off. Yet it meets its target time of 20 days in only 72 per cent of cases.

Hired to undertake a review of the Department of Health, management consultants Coopers and Lybrand compared the efficiency of eight government ministries. They discovered that each Commons question submitted by an MP takes no fewer than 25 civil servants an average of 285 minutes and 79 separate transactions to answer.

Things get worse when it comes to servicing the work of Ministers. The department spends 120 man-hours and £2,693 to prepare for and conduct a single committee meeting. At least three civil servants take the minutes which are then reviewed by six more who amend them, add their comments, then pass them back to the original authors. This takes a total of 53 transactions.

The report, entitled: 'The Review of the Wider Department of Health' identifies a catalogue of inefficiency and waste including committee meetings with nothing to discuss. Junior staff are frustrated at having no responsibility and at having their work repeatedly checked, which actually leads to more errors. Different sections of the department do not know what others are doing and are therefore duplicating tasks. The report concludes: 'There is a suspicion that the presence within the department of a large number of staff itself creates a momentum to develop policy, advice and guidance which can often become a self-justifying activity of little use.'[3]

The benefits of business process improvement

The example above is a classic case where business process improvement is called for. Business process improvement helps organizations structure themselves in a way which is less bureaucratic, more flexible and responsive to customer demands. Among companies that have instituted process redesign programmes in the last few years are Lucas Industries (a pioneer of benchmarking in the mid-1980s with its Competitiveness Achievement Plan for each business unit), National and Provincial Building Society (spurred to change when its plan to become a bank collapsed), Baxi Partnership, Rolls-Royce Cars, Reuters, British Telecom and Rank Xerox UK.

BT and Rank Xerox used the technique as part of their drive to become more customer-focused businesses. The exercise has produced some striking results. For BT, the time to repair private circuits has fallen from five days to five hours; at Rank Xerox the process of special contracts billing which used to take 112 days now takes one day, four hours, 43 minutes. A massive 107 days were saved in one step by cutting out the time that the documents spent in people's in-trays before moving on.[4]

National and Provincial's first year of attacking management hierarchies and bureaucracy produced a double bonus of lower costs and 66 per cent increase in profits despite adverse trading conditions in the mortgage market.

At the heart of process improvement, whatever form it takes, is the achievement of excellent customer service. Organizations which undertake any form of process thinking do so because they believe that the outcome will be more satisfied and loyal customers which in turn will lead to higher levels of profitability.

Baxi Partnership has reduced manufacturing cycle times from nine weeks to 24 hours, cut 18 months out of new product development time and can now make boilers in 52 minutes, rather than six hours. This has resulted in the company maintaining turnover and profitability in a depressed market.

The health insurer, Western Provident Association, has reduced application processing time from 28 days to four days, and settles 90 per cent of claims within five working days. In 1992 its profits were four times higher than they had ever been in the company's history.

By having effective processes in place an organization cuts down the amount of 'fire fighting' which takes place to maintain inefficient systems.

Process thinking brings about improvements in quality and timeliness. It helps cut costs and eliminate waste. It can lead to higher levels of job satisfaction among employees. To improve its competitiveness, British Telecom, for example, plans to cut its costs by 50 per cent through reengineering and develop a process-based competence. The stock-checking system at IBM's personal computer plant in Greenock, Stockend has saved an annual £1.8 million by reengineering its functions to cut out weekend working.

Process thinking can also bring about better relationships between suppliers and their customers. Wal-mart, the hugely successful US supermarket chain, decided to improve its inventory management in one particular area – Pampers baby products – and, by paring down the chain of supply from Proctor and Gamble, eventually ended with P & G taking over the entire inventory management and responsibility for keeping Wal-Mart's shelves stocked.

Wal-Mart has now offloaded a large portion of inventory costs, freed more warehouse space and working capital, and finds its stock replenishment working more smoothly. Inventory management is now so streamlined, in fact, that stock reaches the customer, and is paid for, before Wal-mart has to pay the supplier. For its part, P & G gets 'preferred supplier' status with the chain and spin-off benefits such as prime display positions.[5]

Process thinking therefore is seen to work in the interest of quality, speed, delayering (since lateral thinking attacks the need for vertical hierarchies) and information technology. Although process thinking is often linked to the use of technology it is not always a driver for change. Quite radical changes in organization such as outsourcing support functions in the public sector have not been naturally driven by technology, for example.

There are also less obvious benefits to be gained from business process improvement:

–   In adopting process thinking the organization sends a powerful message to its stakeholders that it is serious in creating a customer focus.

–   When it is undertaken properly, employees feel involved and

recognized as they have an opportunity to identify 'dead wood' and to put suggestions forward for improvement.
–   Process thinking ensures that responsibility is devolved to those people who are most appropriate.
–   Although process thinking does usually facilitate the drive towards empowerment this is not always the case. In some instances, such as the establishment of retail warehouse operations, the new process is capable of de-skilling as much as empowerment. Nevertheless, in general, process thinking necessitates a shift in authority from traditional functional heads to the people responsible for the delivery of the service. In this sense it is different from traditional matrix management.
–   As business process thinking works best when groups of people work together, teamwork can be encouraged and greater understanding and awareness of business needs generated.

Rank Xerox UK used process thinking, for example, to reduce its special billing process from 112 to 24 days, 43 minutes and saved £3 million. When they tackled a key process they saved £11 million. They are so impressed with both the hard and the softer, less tangible outcomes of process improvement, that they are planning to reengineer processes company wide.[6]

 ## Problems and pitfalls of business process improvements

Statistics show that 70 per cent of all process improvement programmes fail. Champy, like Hammer, disputes this underachievement rate. He prefers to say that 30–40 per cent of initiatives 'disappoint'. What cannot be disputed is that many initiatives do run into problems. Some of the most typical causes of failure of business process improvement include:
–   Lack of management ownership/lack of leadership/lack of sponsor.
–   Lack of consideration for customer requirements.
–   Review is targeted on the wrong processes/ lacks strategic relevance/is too narrow in scope.

- Poorly planned review.
- Lack of perseverance or review taking too long to complete.
- Lack of involvement of relevant employees in the review.
- Process improvement not implemented systematically.
- Improvement not sustained by a continuous improvement process.

Let us examine each of these in detail.

Lack of management ownership/lack of leadership/lack of sponsor

The process improvement initiatives undertaken by organizations as far-reaching as Siemens Nixdorf, Pilkington Optronics and Lucas Industries demonstrate that both senior and middle managers are pivotal to the success of business process improvement programmes through the commitment they show to the programme and their leadership of the initiative.

Champy attributes the underachievement or failure of initiatives to managerial block. As we saw in the previous chapter, he argues that the reengineering revolution will never be successful unless it is accompanied by a reengineering of the roles of managers; that is, moving the role of managers from 'command and control' to one of coach and enabler (see Figure 3.1).

Managers may find the enabling role a difficult one to adopt as this new way of working can be seen to threaten their position and authority. As one manager explained: 'I've worked this long and hard to get to this position, I'm not likely now to want to give it all away.'

There is also a commonly held perception among many managers that process improvement involves loss of status,

The old-style manager	The reengineered manager
– Policeofficer	– Coach
– Sets goals	– Defines broad directions
– Defines measures of performance	– Enables others to set performance measures
– Provides outcomes	– Supports outcomes
– Manages others	– Encourages self-management

Figure 3.1 Old style versus reengineered manager

redeployment or even redundancy. This may cause managers reluctance to become involved in a process review. The blunt truth is that many companies who adopt process thinking as a means for change do reduce their management ranks. There is a growing belief that fewer managers make for better managers. Likewise managers may be hesitant to embrace a new way of working which empowers their staff. They may fail to appreciate that by devolving responsibility and encouraging and supporting their staff, managers can gain respect rather than loose status.

In the later chapters we examine how clear objectives, open discussion of fears and barriers, guidance and support of managers can help overcome resistance during a review of processes. It is also particularly important that senior managers devote time to leading and sponsoring the review. Their support needs to be visible and on-going.

Lack of consideration for customer requirements

Process improvement initiatives which are driven by cost saving or for internal, political reasons are less likely to succeed than those where the drive for change is centred on fulfilling customer requirements. This is fundamental to the survival of all businesses. As Peter Drucker says: 'The central task of all business is to get and keep the customer.'

The review is targeted on the wrong processes/ lacks strategic relevance/ is too narrow in scope

Process improvement programmes need to address those processes which are fundamental to business survival. Accepting the idea that businesses are based around two core processes, operations and development, is a fundamental change in mentality for many businesses. Process reviews often go wrong when they are focused on the raft of support processes which complete the organizational structure but which do not add value to the business, and when the core processes on which the subsidiary processes depend are not addressed.

Poorly planned review

As with all change programmes, business process improvement needs effective project management. Later in this book we describe tools and techniques which can be used to facilitate the process. Careful planning and on-going monitoring of performance is particularly key to success.

Lack of perseverance or review taking too long to complete

Once the review has begun, the temptation is to leave the detailed work to others or to begin further initiatives which may be complementary to the programme rather than becoming involved in the detailed implementation of the review. Lack of perseverance or the review taking too long to complete are common causes of failures. This can be attributed to poor leadership, poor project-managing skills and poor teamwork.

Lack of involvement of relevant employees in the review

Change is more acceptable to people when they perceive they have some control over the changes that are to take place. When a review of processes does not involve people who are working on those processes, the consequent improvements are likely to be met with some degree of resistance. As we outline in Chapter 5, the composition of the project team is critical to its success. Likewise the team needs to consult and actively involve people in the review process. In this way they will have a greater understanding of its objectives and likely outcomes.

Process improvement is not implemented systematically

Once recommendations have been made for improvements, the project team usually remains responsible for ensuring that these are acted on systematically. One chain of high street retail outlets, for example, spent much time and effort reviewing its distribution processes. The project team put forward recommendations for a plan of improvements, which in the initial phases was carried out. A year later, a team of management consultants was called in to review the efficiency and effectiveness of the new distribution process. They discovered that the improvements had not been systematically applied. In some cases the new systems were running alongside the old, in others the old processes were still solely in force. When investigating the root causes, the process owners stated that they believed the improvements were too difficult to instigate and that there had been little follow-through, support or encouragement from head office to make the changes work.

Improvement not sustained by a continuous improvement process

A further difficulty often encountered when processes are improved is that the new processes become the accepted company standard. In time they in turn become as rigid, inflexible and unfocused on the customer as the processes they replace. Effective process review, therefore, always includes opportunities for continuous improvements. This is particularly relevant in fast-changing and competitive marketplaces where what become today's standards are outpaced by developments in the future.

 Seven steps to overcome pitfalls

Analysis of organizations who have introduced business process improvements in an effective manner shows that there are seven steps to ensuring the successful implementation of process improvements (see also Figure 3.2).

Step 1. Establish the objectives of the review, its benefits and strategic relevance
An old Chinese proverb states that if you don't know where you are going you are unlikely to get there. A vital first step in the review process is to identify what you are doing and why. Also, clarify how the objectives of the review complement the strategy the organization has developed. It is helpful to set milestones for the review to ensure that it is progressing in the right direction.

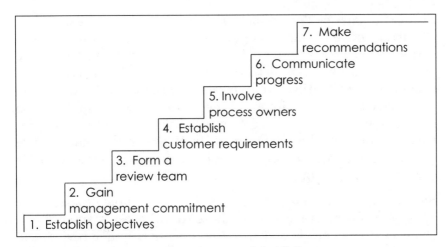

Figure 3.2 Seven steps to overcoming potential pitfalls

Step 2. Get senior management commitment – in words and actions

Senior management need to be actively involved in the process review. Ideally someone from the top of the organization should sponsor the review. They should make clear their expectations of the review and agree working methods and timescales. They need to take an active interest in its progress and be prepared to champion its recommendations among their colleagues.

A survey in 1993, carried out by business consultants Pagoda, of 30 businesses who had started or were in the course of change shows that achieving buy-in is the most critical factor.

Step 3. Form a team of employees who are involved in the process to undertake the review

A team of people should be established to review current processes and to make recommendations on new ways of working. The review team should be led by someone who commands respect in the organization and who has a reputation for getting things done. Likewise the review team's members should be involved in the process they are to improve so they have a good understanding of it. They must have sufficient commitment and command within the organization to ensure that its recommendations are carried through. Importantly, they must be systematic in planning how they will undertake the review and in following through this plan.

Step 4. Canvass customer opinion and establish requirements

The objective of business process improvements should be to better serve the customer. Therefore whoever the customer, be they internal or external to the organization, the review team needs to identify their requirements clearly. They must also establish customers' opinions of the current process and how this can be improved. They need to refer back to customers once an ideal solution has been identified. In this way they can ensure that the improved or new process not only meets but exceeds customer expectations.

Step 5. Canvass the opinion of those involved in the process

The more people involved in the current process understand about customer needs and why the process is under review, the more they are likely to take ownership of the review and support its outcome. There are a number of methods that can be adopted to consult and involve employees in developing new, improved processes. The art is to balance the need for involvement with the need to keep the disruption of current working practices to a minimum.

Step 6. Provide regular updates

Communication is critical in the transition phase of change. When Kingston Hospital, for example, underwent a dramatic reorganization in the way it operated as a hospital, it held regular communication sessions where all members of staff were invited to hear about future plans. These sessions also provided an opportunity for employees to air their concerns and reservations. The communication sessions continued during both the planning and transition phases of the improvements and well into the implementation stage.

Step 7. Make recommendations

The review team needs to use facts and figures to support their findings. When they develop recommendations for improvements they should be aware of the implications for people. Effective teams look for ways of involving employees in the interpretation of findings and minimizing the impact of change through consultation and involvement.

Once improved ways of working have been agreed, the review team need to demonstrate how the new practices will benefit employees. The team will need to consider how to provide employees involved in the new process with training and ongoing support. They also need to put forward recommendations for continual improvement of the new or improved process.

 ## Summary

- In this chapter we outline the benefits of process improvement. The principal benefits are enhanced customer satisfaction and therefore customer retention.
- We describe the problems and pitfalls of implementing business process improvements. Amongst the main barriers identified are the lack of management commitment to the review and lack of focus on customer requirements.
- The chapter concludes by describing seven steps to successful implementation of a process review.

CHAPTER

4

SETTING THE SCENE

Before undertaking a process review, it helps to stand back from the day-to-day effort of organizational life and evaluate fully the marketplace and your organization's position within it. This scene setting can help establish your relative position within the external environment as well as pinpointing practices in the internal organizational environment which may help or hinder the change process. This will give you an insight into conditions which will enable change.

 Enabling conditions

Computer giant ICL is generally recognized as having undertaken a business transformation over the past ten years. In the early 1980s ICL was going through a difficult period. It was purchased by STC for around £20 million. By 1991 the company had undergone a remarkable transformation which resulted in its purchase by Fujitsu who paid over £800 million for an 80 per cent share of ICL. ICL believe that to be successful in reengineering a business you have to create key enabling conditions. These ICL identify as:

– provision of leadership who will share a vision for the way ahead with the organization as a whole;
– flexible human resource practices;
– the willingness to invest in education and training, both extensively and intensively;
– the existence of a readily available IT infrastructure.

ICL set about its corporate transformation by conducting an audit of their business and culture in terms of people, processes and systems. They then established where they wanted to go by adopting four perspectives – to:
1.   execute strategies which align with each other;
2.   become more competitive;
3.   improve operations and service levels, building optimum processes;
4.   exploit the potential of technology.
In this way ICL underpinned its strategic transformation. First ICL embraced strong marketing principles and moved away from being geographically based to being vertically market aligned. Next it implemented an 'investing in people' programme designed to ensure that every member of staff had clear objectives, was rewarded for performance and was developed in a systematic way.

ICL examined their manufacturing processes and changed two key things. Instead of trying to innovate everything as they used to do, they started to purchase best-of-breed from other suppliers and incorporated it into their own designs. They implemented just-in-time manufacturing processing throughout their assembly plants.

The final area to note is that in the mid-1980s ICL embarked on the quality trail, embracing quality and endeavouring to build a zero defect culture into the key business processes. They have also embarked on an extensive customer care programme in order to provide a strategic edge in the market.[7]

Undertake an audit of where you are now

Like ICL, to prepare for business transformation through process improvement successful organizations often undertake an audit to better understand where they are and what they are doing. The audit can be carried out from both an external and an internal perspective.

External environment

It is useful to have an understanding of your organization's position within the marketplace so that you can gauge where it stands in relation to external forces. This analysis can be carried out by a project team who will subsequently work in redesigning organizational processes.

Here is a checklist of likely questions which we suggest are considered in a preliminary review (see also Figure 4.1):

1. What marketplace does your organization operate in? (A restaurant chain can be said to be operating in the leisure market, a pen manufacturer can be seen as operating in the gift market, for example.)
2. Who are your customers? (Break these down as far as possible by type of customer, retention rate, etc.)
3. What is the skill set required to meet customer demands?
4. What are the attitudes/behaviours required to meet customer needs?
5. What image do your customers have of your company's products and services?
6. What is your company's unique selling point or competitive advantage?
7. Describe the state of the marketplace: its size, growth, price sensitivity, time sensitivity, quality sensitivity.
8. What are the likely changes in the marketplace in the short term?
9. What are the changes likely to affect the marketplace in the long term?
10. What is the availability of suppliers?
11. Who are your competitors?
12. What is their share of the market?
13. What is the trend in terms of their market share?
14. What is your share of the market?
15. Is this share increasing/decreasing or remaining static?
16. What has been your company's financial performance for the last year/five years?
17. What is your company's price position as seen relative to the competition?
18. What is your company's degree of profitability?
19. What is the cashflow position of your company?

Once you have answered these questions, it helps to summarize the outcome/your perceptions by producing a SWOT analysis of the results. This itemizes your perceptions of your company's strengths, weaknesses, opportunities facing the organization and threats.

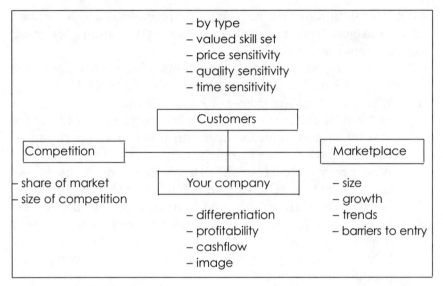

Figure 4.1 Understanding the external environment

Strengths	Weaknesses
Opportunities	Threats

Figure 4.2 Example of SWOT analysis grid

As a general rule, strengths and weaknesses will be inherent in the company whereas opportunities and threats present themselves from outside the company. For example, external forces which threaten the organization could include competitive new product development, while opportunities may be, for example, growth of demand in new market areas.

It is normal to summarize the SWOT analysis in grid format, as shown in Figure 4.2.

Internal analysis

An audit of the external environment will not be sufficient in itself. A company's performance is also governed by internal factors which it is beneficial to understand. Put simply, the task is to review how the organization is structured in terms of the managerial, operational, social and technological (MOST) aspects.

As a precursor to launching a business process improvement project, therefore, it is expedient to fully understand the working environment in which this is to take place. Business process improvement is not a panacea for business ills nor does it promise instant transformation from mediocrity into excellence. Business process improvement can provide a valuable framework for organizational change but only when the organization puts in place a structure to motivate, pay and inspire people to perform a process to the customer's satisfaction.

Before undertaking a process review, therefore, effective project teams ask themselves this series of key questions:

What is the vision of the organization?
- Is it appropriate in today's environment?
- When was it last reviewed?
- Is it a commonly held vision or one which has been developed and is shared only by the senior management team?
- Is the vision perceived to be achievable or purely a fantasy of how things should be in the organization?

Organizations who successfully embrace change, such as British Airways, review their vision and mission statement every three to five years to ensure that it is still appropriate.

Many organizations involve their employees in the development of a vision. One large insurance company, for example, invited its employees to a series of workshops where people from different parts of the organization took part in a 'visioning exercise'. They were handed tools for drawing and colouring, pulls from magazines and newspapers, and invited to put together a graphic representation of the vision of how they perceived the organization should be in three years time. Perhaps not unsurprisingly, a set of common pictures emerged. Employees at all levels depicted a flatter, more team-orientated organization which was closer to the customer. They saw themselves at the forefront of the marketplace, the envy of their competitors because of their outstanding levels of customer service. From this series of workshop activities a shared vision was determined for the organization. This was commonly understood and agreed as its development had been shared by employees.

Once a clear and shared vision for the organization's future has been developed it is possible to establish the degree of change needed to achieve this vision by determining a gap between the current organizational performance and the desired vision for the future. A vision statement is normally no longer than a paragraph and is written in a language everyone can understand. Here are some examples of vision statements from a variety of organizations:

- A Japanese car manufacturer: 'To supply products of the highest quality, yet at a reasonable price for worldwide customer service'.
- A telecommunications company: 'To set the standard for customer care in the UK, always working to develop products and systems tailored to the individual needs of our customers'.
- An investment bank: 'To be the world's leading investment bank and the first choice for our clients, employees and shareholders'.
- A double glazing company: 'To maintain market leadership by achieving unrivalled reputation in our industry for exceptional customer care'.

What are the values of the organization?
As opposed to a vision, which sets out the purpose and aims of an organization, values describe what the company believes in, what the company stands for and the expected pattern of behaviour of its employees.

The social infrastructure of an organization is often based on the values it expounds. One company, for example, identified four key values which underpinned their way of doing business:

- Integrity.
- Customer service.
- Teamwork.
- Open communication.

In establishing an organization's values it is helpful to bear in mind there is often a difference between theory and practice. The

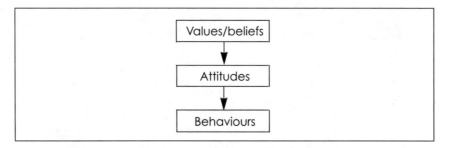

Figure 4.3 How values/belief systems affect behaviour

value of 'open communication' can be an illustration of this. It is often one of the key values of many organizations, yet in practice many workers may believe that improvements could be enforced in this area.

What are typical behaviours of employees in the company?
An indication of the true state of the values of an organization can be obtained by looking at the behaviour of its employees. Firefighting, stressful working patterns, long hours and little sharing or personal support for example, may be at odds with the published values of an organization. These behaviours do not reflect a customer mindedness or feeling of teamwork.

What attitudes do your employees display?
Behaviour in the workplace often affects employees' attitudes and belief systems (Figure 4.3).

The attitude people adopt is often confirmed by their behaviour towards the customers. I went into a shop recently to purchase a product. As the layout of the shop was unfamiliar, I asked one of two assistants behind the counter for the product. The assistants were deep in conversation and barely made eye contact with me. They pointed in the direction of the shelves and, although there were no other customers in the shop, neither was prepared to finish their conversation to help me.

When I returned to the counter to pay, the assistants were again very dismissive. They continued their discussion, ignoring me completely. In fact their conversation centred on the way they had been treated by their manager, the long hours and low pay. They made no attempt to hide their own dissatisfaction from me and I left the shop very dissatisfied.

Current attitude	Need to move to
– That customer service means 'not selling'	– Ability to exploit selling opportunities
– 0830 – 1630 as time when company is 'open'	– Extend 'open' hours through shifts + service to customer
– Fear of change/progress	– Encourage initiatives/empowerment
– Lack of 'buzz'	– Display genuine enthusiasm
– Customers are all external	– Care of internal 'customers'

Figure 4.4 Example of current and desired attitudes

Often, therefore, to provide excellent customer service the attitudes and value systems of employees throughout an organization need to be changed as part of a process improvement exercise.

Figure 4.4 is an example of one organization's assessment of employees' attitude and where they need to change.

How would you describe your organization's 'corporate culture'?
Employees' attitudes are influenced by many factors in the organization's culture. One of the key criteria of success in any change programme is to decide what factors in corporate culture provide strength to the organization and which factors need to change.

There may be many aspects of an organization's traditional paradigms – belief system, associations or ways of thinking which are held as common and taken for granted – which are beneficial, others may act as a hindrance to achieving the organization's vision.

Corporate culture is evident in a number of different aspects of organizational life.

Factors which provide evidence of an organization's culture (see also Figure 4.5) include:
– *Physical appearance:* how people dress to come to work, the props they use at work, for example briefcases, filofaxes, pens, etc. In one software company which is a subsidiary of a US parent, male executives wear white Oxford button-down shirts, dark suits, blue ties, brogues (black only) and if they wear glasses they must be designer labels! Their dress is modelled on their US counterparts, even though the UK

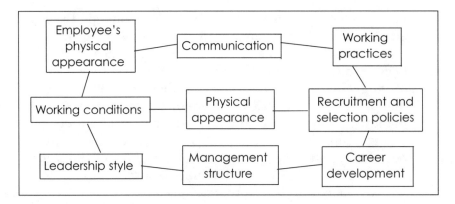

Figure 4.5 Examples of evidence of corporate culture

   senior managers are British, as the prevailing cultural belief equates this appearance with success.
– *Working conditions:* length of hours worked, flexitime, outsourcing, performance related pay – these are examples which will vary from firm to firm but which influence the corporate climate.
– *Physical environment:* open-plan or closed offices, plants and pictures or bare walls, hot desking, rest areas. We all know that physical environment influences people's behaviour. One London firm of management consultants have a policy of hot desking in its offices, the offices are streamlined and very modern in appearance. There are no decorations or plants in evidence. Hard work and efficiency are the order of the day.
– *Communications:* both written and spoken communications are also evidence of an organization's culture – for example, the use of E-mail, internal correspondence, internal briefing and feedback mechanisms.
– *Working practices:* the formality or lack of formality of working practices, the degree of responsibility and empowerment.
– *Recruitment and selection processes, career development:* will influence people's expectation of the job and hence their behaviour. One firm of accountants, for example, have traditionally recruited only graduates of the highest calibre. Their culture is one of meritocracy, where career progression is governed by achievement within the firm.

Partners are very rarely brought in from outside the firm. Until recently there have been very few women in senior management positions. These factors influence employees' loyalty to the firm and their behaviours.

– *Management structure:* the number and hierarchy of managers, the qualities an organization requires of its managers. One pub chain, for example, deliberately puts young people into positions of authority. It has few levels between a pub manager and senior members of the boards. It fosters an energetic and dynamic culture, where there are ample opportunities for progression.

– *Management style:* there is an old saying 'happy staff means happy customers'. The way people are managed influences their own attitudes Where, as in some organizations, management attitudes prevail that employees are basically untrustworthy, this belief will probably become a self-fulfilling prophecy. If attitudes exist such as this, the main part of the business process improvement programme should be to focus on removing redundant, internally focused control processes.

What is the quality of the leadership of the organization?
Effective leaders set a strong direction for their organization and provide a framework in which their followers can operate. They inspire and energize their workers and focus the organization on a common set of objectives. Strong leaders are needed in times of change to champion the cause of change and to successfully manage the transition.

When British Airways began a process of corporate transformation its chief executive set out a clear path for change. He championed the need to change and spent much of his time communicating this need.

What are the objectives of the organization?
– Are these objectives in line with the corporate vision?
– Are the objectives well known throughout the organization?
– Are they specific, measurable and achievable?
– Does each part of the business set specific goals?
Food retailer Tesco involves all its top team in the development of corporate objectives. The objectives are cascaded through to each of its stores which in turn sets local goals. Regular

communication meetings are held to feed back to managers how well the organization is progressing towards its goal.

What strategy is the organization currently adopting to achieve its goals?
–   Is this strategy appropriate?
–   Is it bringing results?

The strategy adopted by computer software giant Microsoft to achieve its corporate goals, for example, was one of acquisition. Its approach is to buy up or buy in skills and knowledge which will help it stay ahead of the competition. Coupled with aggressive new product development, this has ensured the company is a leader in its field.

What is the structure of the organization?
–   How many layers are there between the top and the bottom of the organization?
–   Is the organization structured on a functional or process basis?
–   Is teamwork encouraged?
–   Does the way the company is currently structured help or impede its attainment of goals?

What degree of involvement have employees in the decision-making process?
–   Are there opportunities for continuous improvement?
–   Is there a mechanism in place for employees to put forward their ideas?
–   How well is this used?
–   What degree of ownership is there for improvements throughout the organization?

How well does the organization communicate internally?
–   What is the mechanism for communicating from senior management downwards?
–   How is information fed back?
What opportunities are there for career development?
–   How is performance managed?
–   What are the success criteria for promotion?
–   How is the succession process managed?
–   What responsibility does the individual have for their own career development?
–   What training and development opportunities are available?

Attitude surveys can help pinpoint the strengths and weaknesses apparent in an organization's culture through the beliefs expressed by its employees. Surveys normally begin with focus groups when the project team can obtain a qualitative view of the issues facing the organization. Following on from the groups it is normal for a questionnaire to be designed to gain quantitative data. Usually a questionnaire consists of statements or pairs of statements designed to gauge employees' opinions. Employees who complete the questionnaires do so in confidence and are asked to indicate their degree of agreement with the statements, from strong agreement through to disagreement, on a scale of 1 to 5.

Questions can cover a wide range of topic areas such as employees' attitudes towards customers, communication within the organization, understanding of roles and responsibilities, teamwork and empowerment, recognition and employee care, career and training opportunities, understanding of organizational aims.

Figure 4.6 shows the type of questions that can be asked in a survey where employees are asked to rate their degree of agreement or disagreement to each statement. Normally statements are jumbled up within a questionnaire. Once the questionnaires have been completed it is then possible to analyse the results and gain a better understanding of the culture of an organization.

Creating a SWOT analysis

Once you have undertaken the internal audit it is helpful to summarize the findings into a SWOT analysis. Although this analysis may be purely subjective, both this and the external analysis serve as a useful opportunity for understanding the organization and its environment better. This awareness will help project team members as they investigate and redesign processes. In particular it will acquaint project team members with some of the soft issues which need to be addressed in bringing about change and how best to manage these.

- I am encouraged to suggest new ideas.
- Improvements are shared between one department/team and another.
- New ideas are put into action.
- People work together to solve problems jointly.
- Teamwork is good within the organization.
- I find out what is happening through the grapevine.
- I am usually told quickly of key changes/developments which affect the business.
- Communication is open throughout the organization.
- My roles and responsibilities are clear.
- I understand the objectives of the organization and the part I have to play in achieving them.
- I know the priorities/objectives of my team.
- I can generally give customers what they want.
- The customer is the most important person in our business.
- I am usually able to solve customer problems/difficulties.
- I am given adequate praise and recognition for a job well done.
- The organization values its people and looks after me.
- My manager encourages me to develop.
- There is ample opportunity for career development within the organization.
- I am given adequate training to do my job properly.
- My training and development needs are regularly reviewed.
- Managers provide me with the support I need to do my job well.
- There are too many rules in the organization.
- I can work in a flexible fashion to meet customer demands.
- The organization needs to change to stay ahead.
- It would be best if my job stayed the same.

Figure 4.6 Example of questions designed to gauge employee attitudes

Summary

- This chapter outlines the steps to be taken before launching a business process improvement programme.
- It is worthwhile undertaking a review or audit of both external and internal factors in the organization's working environment before beginning a process review.
- The chapter sets out a checklist of factors to be analysed in the external environment.

- It also identifies areas for analysis within the organization to help the members of the review team gain a better understanding of the cultural issues affecting the organization. Employee attitude surveys are a useful barometer.

THE FOUR-STAGE APPROACH

This chapter provides an overview of the stages of business process improvement.

Irrespective of the scale of the improvement to current processes that is undertaken, be it process improvement, process redesign or business process reengineering, there are four distinct stages that need to be completed. These are shown in Figure 5.1.

The four stages of process improvement correspond to the Plan–Do–Check–Act cycle.

– *Plan*   corresponds to Stage 1 – identifying processes in need of improvement. Here the project team must gain a good understanding of the organization's current processes which are in need of improvement. The objectives of the review must be defined and opportunities for improvement pinpointed. Customer requirements need to be established.

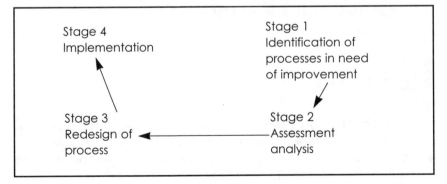

Figure 5.1 Overview of the four stages of process improvement

– *Do*   incorporates Stage 2 – assessment and analysis of the chosen processes. The team collects data on the current process and makes an assessment of its strengths and weaknesses, opportunities for improvement and potential areas of threat.

– *Check* ⎫ involves Stages 3 – process redesign and 4 –
– *Act*   ⎭ implementation.

–   Stage 3 – the redesign of processes is where new ways of working are formulated which better meet customer requirements. Recommendations are put forward for improvement and quick wins identified.

–   Stage 4 involves the implementation of recommendations. Here progress is monitored according to measures. New processes are corrected, maintained, improved.

Typically a review of processes will involve 60 per cent effort in Stages 1, 2 and 3 and 40 per cent in Stage 4 – the critical implementation phase.

 ## Overview of activities in each stage of the cycle

Within each stage of the four-part review cycle are a number of discrete activities. Figure 5.2 sets out tools and techniques which can be used to facilitate progress in each stage of the cycle.

The following chapters set out a detailed plan of each stage in the process review cycle and describe the tools which can be used to conduct the activities in each stage.

 ## Summary

- This chapter provides an overview of the four stages of process redesign and the activities involved in each stage.
- It sets out a master list of the tools that can be used to facilitate each stage in the cycle.

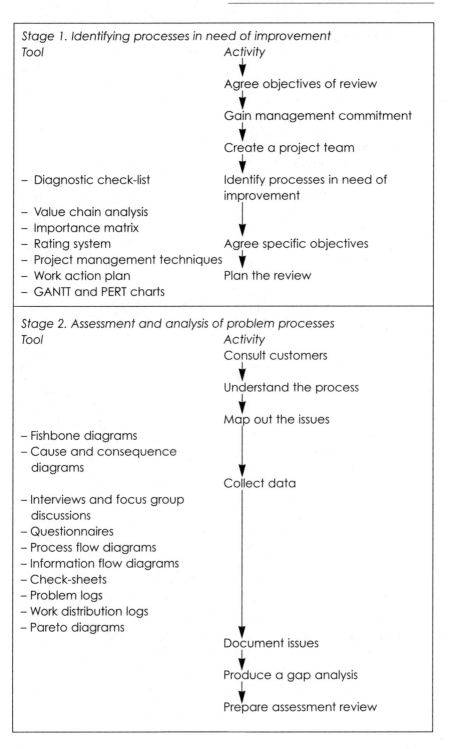

Stage 1. *Identifying processes in need of improvement*
Tool   *Activity*

                                        Agree objectives of review

                                        Gain management commitment

                                        Create a project team

– Diagnostic check-list   Identify processes in need of
                                        improvement
– Value chain analysis
– Importance matrix
– Rating system   Agree specific objectives
– Project management techniques
– Work action plan   Plan the review
– GANTT and PERT charts

Stage 2. *Assessment and analysis of problem processes*
Tool   *Activity*
                                        Consult customers

                                        Understand the process

                                        Map out the issues
– Fishbone diagrams
– Cause and consequence
  diagrams
                                        Collect data
– Interviews and focus group
  discussions
– Questionnaires
– Process flow diagrams
– Information flow diagrams
– Check-sheets
– Problem logs
– Work distribution logs
– Pareto diagrams

                                        Document issues

                                        Produce a gap analysis

                                        Prepare assessment review

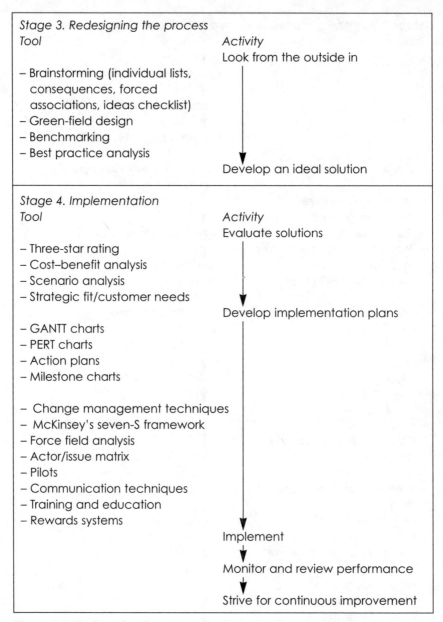

Figure 5.2 Tools and techniques to facilitate the Plan–Do–Check–Act cycle

CHAPTER

6

STAGE 1: IDENTIFYING THE NEEDS

This chapter deals with the important planning stages of the review:
– What should be the objectives of the review?
– How do you gain management commitment?
– How to create a project team.
– Which processes are in need of improvement?
– Agreeing milestones.
– Planning the review.

Agreeing the objectives of the review

The first step in any business processing improvement programme should be the setting of clear objectives for the review. For example, one organization identified as its main objective as to bring about incremental change in the range of 20–25 per cent in one of its core processes – post sales service – where it sought performance improvements to bring it ahead of its competitors.

Another organization, the American fast food chain outlet Taco Bell set an objective of reducing everything but the cost of goods sold in order to compete in a marketplace where other competitors spent millions of dollars in marketing their businesses. This decision called for a total change of attitude to paradigms within the company. This involved step change brought about through a business process reengineering project.

Other businesses have set themselves objectives for transformational change programmes such as 'to create a more customer-focused environment'. Often process thinking is one mechanism in achieving this aim.

The preparation outlined in the last chapter will help, therefore, to set objectives for the programme. In particular understanding the DNA of an organization's culture – what are its beliefs, rules and regulations, communications, history, overt and hidden agendas, stories and myths, reward systems, products and services, offices and buildings, will help the project team identify how the organization views change. In addition, it is helpful to understand what degree of change the individuals on the board of a company will tolerate, and their degree of commitment to change on an ongoing basis.

In 1989 a new chief executive named David Dry joined Baxi, the old-established Preston firm of domestic boiler and heater manufacturers. He found a company embarked on what it considered a progressive and motivated course, to transform itself from a family firm into a share-owning partnership. It was doing well enough but serious problems loomed on the horizon, including a slowdown of market growth, rising costs that consequently could not be absorbed and changes among boiler competitors and customers that threatened Baxi's market share and profit margins.

Dry saw the main problem was a top-down one: there was no effective shared vision of the key issues, and the company suffered from a serious cultural block. The staff of 1,000 were not being used to their full potential, nor was the company structured to drive future business success in areas such as productivity, quality and speed of innovation. What was required was radical and irreversible change.

Dry deliberately pushed through a remarkable 'big bang'.

The company was divided into six self-governing business areas, with some activities retained as central services (corporate accounting, sales, procurement, management information systems and IT, long-term R&D and central engineering). Its new management structure resembled a wheel, with the board in the centre, circled respectively with business area leaders and an outer layer of team leaders.

The directors switched from their old responsibilities for functions such as marketing and finance with responsibility for portfolios of business areas and specialist functions.

On the shop-floor multi-skilled teams broke down old demarcations and 'them and us' attitudes, pushed up quality and productivity, identified more closely with product and customer and in general helped to drive the programme from the bottom up. It was a complete reversal of the top-down culture.

Results have been extremely successful yet Dry is now out of a job. Ironically, the board that had so eagerly embraced his vision of change found that, in Dry's words, they had a 'tiger by the tail'.[8]

The lesson learnt is that senior management do not always appreciate the full implications of a successful reengineering programme. Once commitment is gained from shop-floor and middle management the demands roll back on the board. Senior managers may be left exposed if their own commitment is less than iron clad.

The moral is that the board should never underestimate the challenge of reengineering, especially in a company that may be doing respectably well.

 ## Gaining commitment

Senior management must be committed to business process improvement before a review takes place. Ideally the sponsor of the review should be a member of senior management. He or she needs to champion the improvements and link these to solid business objectives.

The board of a business is likely to be won over by the benefits they will derive from a review of processes in terms of improved performance. Not only do they need a clear understanding of the stages involved in a review and the resources required for its completion, they also should be encouraged to take an active interest in the review so that they understand how it is progressing.

An example of a business process reengineering study which has been championed from the top is Anglian Water's initiative. When the water industry was privatized, each of the new companies inherited the legacy of years of under-funding, ministerial interference and short-term decision making. Alan

Smith, Group Managing Director of Anglian Water (AW) had been in the top job since April 1990 and was well aware of the need for change. But he did not want to begin too fast. The transfer of some 1,200 staff to the National Rivers Authority, just before privatization, had already caused one major reorganization and he was anxious to avoid further upheaval. 'For the first two or three years, we decided to keep things as they were and focus on the main objective of managing our compliance with the water quality requirements', Smith says. More drastic action would have to come later.

By 1992 that moment had arrived. Smith identified three key objectives: customer focus; commitment to total quality; and efficiency.

Smith proposed a Strategic Systems Review (SSR) – a classic business process reengineering study focused on office-based activities. In January 1993 a team of independent consultants was commissioned to work with six of Anglia Water's top managers to examine every aspect of the white-collar side of the business, from logistics and finance to human resources and water quality science. The team also visited some 250 companies in Europe and the US to look at best practice in a host of other industries and markets.

Fundamental to the changes was the introduction of a far flatter management structure comprising just five layers from top to bottom. 'The idea was that there should be only three tiers between any individual and the top', says Smith.

Another crucial change involved moving away from the command-and-control style of management that had prevailed in the past. Existing management practices were effective but not particularly efficient and caused widespread dissatisfaction among staff – a fact which became overwhelmingly apparent when Smith canvassed his staff for their views on the company's management style in an employee opinion survey in June 1993.

Smith seized the opportunity to get all his senior managers to commit to a more open style of management. Anyone who opposed the move had to go. As a first step, he decided to hold a series of employee presentations on the results of the survey. 'It was an embarrassing experience getting up in front of all those people and reading out strongly-worded negative comments on subjects such as my salary', he says. But he is convinced that for many employees those presentations were a turning-point. 'Until that moment many of them did not believe that the changes we had been talking about would happen.'[9]

Further down the organization it is helpful to create a general understanding of external forces which drive the business towards change. In this way resistance to change may be eliminated. Likewise it is useful to create an understanding of the expectations of customers. One car manufacturer, for example, regularly invites its shop-floor workers to attend consumer research panels. In this way it hopes to create an awareness of how the product is used and why.

Although only a small number of people will initially be involved in a process review, experience shows that it is best to adopt a participative approach to the study. This means involving as many people as possible in the project through explaining its objectives and asking for contributions. Although employees will not be aware of the finer details of the project, they should at best have an understanding of its aims and benefits. Team briefings are a helpful mechanism for disseminating this form of information.

 Forming a project team

Having gained management commitment and a sponsor for the review, the next step is to form a project team headed by a project leader.

Ideally, the team should consist of managers and staff who are both users and owners of the process under review and where possible their internal customers plus other people who can take an impartial overview of the process. The ideal number is six to eight in a project team. Remember to select participants who have the influence/knowledge/capacity to complete the task and who bring a wide range of perspective to the team.

Before the project commences with the first stage of review, it is useful to establish roles and general rules for the team. For example:
–   What is the objective of the project?
–   To what timescale is the project team working?
–   When will the team meetings take place and how frequently?

- Who will chair the discussion? (Should this be the project leader or will there be a rotating chair?)
- Who will take minutes and how detailed should these be?
- Should there be an agenda for each meeting?

Do not expect the team to get down to the task in hand immediately. Every team goes through a 'getting to know each other' phase. Challenge in a team can be healthy. In particular, team members should be encouraged to 'think out of the box' and to question existing working practices. Team-building events or training workshops held shortly after the team is first formed can help the team get to know each other.

There are a variety of diagnostic tools which will help team members identify the strengths they bring to the team. Belbin, for example, established nine team types:

- *The implementer:* a practical person who likes to get things done.
- *The co-ordinator:* co-ordinates the team and facilitates progress towards its goals.
- *The ideas person (plant):* puts forward original ideas.
- *The resource instigator:* good at finding resources in the external environment.
- *The monitor evaluator:* evaluates ideas and proposals and monitors the progress of the team.
- *The completer/finisher:* concerned with detail; likes to dot the i's and cross the t's.
- *The driver (shaper):* shapes the way the team works and can provide motivation and encouragement.
- *The team worker:* quieter member of the team who is keen to promote team spirit.
- *The specialist:* brings specialist knowledge to the team.

Belbin explains that everyone has a preferred type of role to play in a team. Each type has strengths and weaknesses.

An effective team consists of a group of people, with complementary roles, who have a common goal and who recognize that it takes the efforts of each one of the team members to achieve that goal.

The four cornerstones to good teamwork (summarized in Figure 6.1) are:

Trust

Team members need to trust each other. They need to have confidence that their team-mates will do what they say they will

Trust	Support
Communication	Commitment

Figure 6.1 The four cornerstones of effective teamwork

do and that they can share information in confidence with all members of the team.

Support
Team members must be able to rely on the personal support of their colleagues. This ensures that the work is shared and problems are openly acknowledged and solved in a collective fashion.

Communication
Good communication is vital in an effective team. People need to know what is to happen and why, they need to be able to discuss and share experiences and to understand individual responsibilities.

Commitment
A team will not function well unless it is committed to a set of common aims.

The role of the chairperson is particularly influential. He or she should be responsible for actively involving all team members in discussion, for planning each meeting and ensuring responsibilities are allocated for activities which are to take place in preparation for the subsequent meeting – and that these responsibilities are carried through. Recording ideas during the meeting, summarizing and restating views also ensures that meetings are well managed and that everyone's contributions are acknowledged.

Finally, during the course of a series of meetings, a good chairperson takes five minutes on a frequent basis to review the effectiveness of the team process. In this way blockages to effective teamwork can be identified and improvements made to how the team works together.

One method of inviting feedback is to ask each member of the team to score various aspects of the team process on a scale of 1 to 5, where 1 = very poor, 2 = poor, 3 = average, 4 = good, 5 = very good. An example is as follows:

– Understanding by all team members of team objectives.
– Communication within the team.
– Decision making within the team.
– Degree of encouragement and support given to team members.
– Degree to which team members feel included in the team.
– Extent to which the strengths of individual members are used within the team.
– Extent to which disagreement and conflict is acknowledged within the team.

Once each team member has completed a rating a general discussion can take place on the collective scores and the reason for these. In this way areas for improvement can be identified.

Identifying processes in need of improvement

There is divergence of opinion on what constitutes the 'core' business processes – the critical processes that will determine organizational success. Some organizations have applied the concept to the interpretation of all tasks relating to the business activities that form part of the 'critical success factors' such as supplier chain management, new product development, stock control, cost management, delivery, etc. Others focus on activities relating to different product streams, still others define processes in terms of activities relating to products and services offered to customer segments.

The starting-point for the project team should be to identify the organization's core processes. In this way processes in need of improvement can be prioritized and their importance categorized in line with the organization's strategic objectives.

Mercury, the telecommunications company, for example, has identified 33 groups of processes. Xerox have identified ten core processes and a further 53 secondary ones. Once processes are known, those which are fundamental to the business can be analysed to bring about improvements.

A simple method of identifying processes in need of improvement is to hold a brainstorming session. Here team

members can compile a list of processes which:
- cause most complaints to external and/or internal customers;
- cause most errors;
- take most time to complete;
- involve most people;
- involve least people/depend on a few key individuals;
- do not engender ownership/responsibility/answerability;
- involve duplication of effort;
- incur most costs.

When a list of processes has been established through brainstorming the team needs to agree which ones are the most important to be reviewed. Here are a number of methodologies that can be adopted: diagnostic check-list, value chain analysis, importance matrix and rating system.

Diagnostic check-list

The diagnostic check-list (Figure 6.2) sets out a list of symptoms which are indicative of ineffective processes. Rate the processes you have chosen and then evaluate the score for each process.

Value chain Analysis

Another technique which can be used to identify processes in need of improvement is to understand fully a business's value chain.

All activities in a business can be seen as a series of steps which add value to the customer. If the final price paid by the customer is 100 per cent, it is possible to work back through the steps in the process through which the customer receives the product or service. The value of each activity can then be calculated as a percentage of the total cost to the customer (see Figure 6.3).

Using this analysis companies can find ways of improving individual processes – in this instance the warehousing activity – or in restructuring the way value is added to the client.

A textile manufacturer examined the activities involved in producing one of its top-selling product lines. Out of a total of 30

	Yes	No
Customers		
1. Do customers complain of poor service?	——	——
2. Can improvements be made to service providers' knowledge of customer needs?	——	——
3. Do errors occur more frequently than in 10% of cases?	——	——
4. Do customers return your product through dissatisfaction?	——	——
5. Are you losing customers because of dissatisfaction?	——	——
6. Is there duplication of effort by staff who provide the service to the customer?	——	——
Activities		
7. Are there multiple steps in the activities involved in delivering the product or service to the customer?	——	——
8. Do backlogs frequently occur in the process?	——	——
9. Does the process involve large amounts of paperwork?	——	——
People		
10. Does the process involve large amount of people in different locations?	——	——
11. Does the process depend on key information or individuals?	——	——
12. Does the process involve staff spending large amounts of time in problem solving?	——	——
13. Is the morale of staff working on the process low?	——	——
14. Do staff working on the process spend longer hours than their counterparts in other areas of the business?	——	——
15. Is there little involvement of staff in identifying areas for improvement in the process?	——	——
Data		
16. Is data collected in the process from different systems?	——	——
17. Is data collected in the process which is of little use?	——	——
18. Is data collected during the process which is out of date?	——	——
Outcomes		
19. Does the process perform less well than it is targeted to do?	——	——
20. Is the process frequently over budget in terms of cost?	——	——

Scoring
Total the number of yeses you have marked.

Score out of 20 _____

How to interpret your scores	
12 or more yeses	Your process is in need of a thorough review. Radical process redesign may be called for.
6–11 yeses	Your process displays many of the symptoms of one which needs improvement.
1–5 yeses	It appears that your process works relatively effectively. Use the checklist to identify any potential areas for improvement.

Figure 6.2 The diagnostic check-list

purchasing raw materials	→ production	→ warehousing	→ marketing	→ distribution
10%	35%	39%	6%	10%

Figure 6.3 Example of a simple value chain for a manufacturing company

activities only six added value. On average 10 per cent of the total manufacturing time was accounted for by value-added operations. The customer, therefore, was paying for 90 per cent of the time the product was in storage, queuing in front of machines, in transit around the factory or being inspected. Measurement of the non-value added elements proved a useful technique in identifying assessing performance and pinpointing areas for improvement in work in progress, transit and overtime worked.

Importance matrix

This tool provides a speedy means of evaluating the importance and critical nature of a process. Draw a matrix with importance on one axis and criticality on the other (Figure 6.4). The importance axis represents the importance of the process to customer satisfaction. The criticality matrix represents how critical the process is to achieving the organization's strategy.

Next, decide where to position each process on the importance/critical matrix. For example, a food manufacturing company identified four processes in need of improvement: delivery, new product development, supplier selection and team briefing. (Figure 6.5). Plotting each process on the importance/critical matrix demonstrates their importance to customer satisfaction

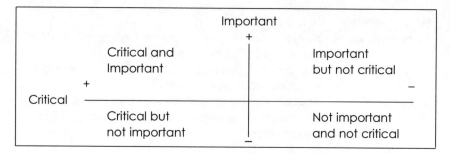

Figure 6.4 Example of an importance/critical matrix

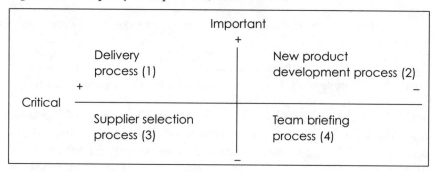

Figure 6.5 Example of a completed importance/critical matrix

and how essential the process is to the company's strategy. Therefore, the process which is important and critical, in this case delivery, should be tackled first.

Rating system

An alternative method of selecting the most important process to improve is to use a rating system. Here each process is marked on a scale of 1 (low) to 5 (high) against different criteria, as in Figure 6.6. The criteria used must be agreed by all the project team members.

In addition to those illustrated in the example, other criteria which can be used as the basis of a decision include:
– delay;
– backlogs;
– amount of data to be processed;
– duplication of effort;
– amount of time spent problem solving.

Process	Complaints	Criteria Errors	Time	People	Effort involved	Cost	Total out of 30
	(1-5)	(1-5)	(1-5)	(1-5)	(1-5)	(1–5)	
Delivery	4	4	4	3	4	5	24
New product development	3	2	4	4	4	4	21
Supplier selection	2	2	4	3	4	3	18
Team briefing	4	2	2	4	4	1	17

Figure 6.6 Example of a rating system for a food manufacturing company

 ## Project management tools

Organizations such as the pharmaceuticals company Glaxo Wellcome have recognized that in the fast-moving competitive environment it is important that planning for change is both competitive and swift. Glaxo, together with many other businesses who use process thinking as a tool for change, have developed and trained their staff in a project management methodology which allows it to plan and implement change in a more efficient fashion.

Many project teams find it useful, therefore, to undergo training in project management techniques, particularly when the process under review is complex and when the team involved is drawn from fairly disparate functions. The danger of adopting too formal project management techniques is that they can become too inflexible and bureaucratic. The tools, therefore, should be used to facilitate the review process, not to hinder it.

There are a number of steps to be taken at the beginning of a process review.

Setting objectives

In order to clarify initial understandings, once you have agreed as a team which process to review, remember to set specific objectives for the study. For example, the project team who undertook to review the delivery process for the food manufacturing company set itself the following objectives:

> To undertake a review of the delivery process of finished goods from the factory to customers' premises in order to improve the process in terms of time, accuracy and quality and thereby improve customer satisfaction. The review to be completed within six months and recommendations to be made to the Board by November.

The objectives set for the team should be SMART:
–   Specific;
–   Measurable;
–   Achievable;
–   Realistic timescale.

Air Products sees project definition as one of the key phases in any reengineering project. Air Products applied a variety of methods to manage this phase in two simultaneous reengineering projects, one in the UK and one in the US. They developed a methodology which helped the steering committees define the scope of the project, identify the trigger and finishing points of the process and establish relevant goals and performance measures.

Other organizations set themselves strict measures of success. GEC Alsthom set itself strict criteria when it undertook a process redesign. These included:
–   achievement of main business objectives;
–   no relocation of factory;
–   no closure of factory.

British Gas has had a number of quality initiatives running in recent years. Their total quality approach places great emphasis on people and processes, customer requirements and expectations.

Their 'top down' approach to total quality involves each unit, no matter what size, developing their own mission and goals in support of the corporate business objectives. Critical success factors are then identified to achieve these goals, together with a list of key supporting business processes. These are prioritized in terms of criticality and current efficiency in order to decide a sequence in which to work on them. Finally, project teams are formed to improve the processes, with a good understanding of which processes are to be improved and why. Benchmarking against the best in other organizations is increasingly becoming part of British Gas's improvement toolbox. This helped British Gas identify more radical means of change in response to the Monopoly and Mergers Commission call for drastic changes in the way British Gas operates.

Identify the customer and potential benefits

A further step is to set out a description of the business reasons for performing the review and to estimate the potential impact of the work. Here the project team should agree:
1. Who is the ultimate customer or end user of the process?
2. What are customers' needs?
3. What are the problems associated with the current process?
4. What opportunities are there the better to meet customer needs?
5. How might the customer benefit as a result of the review?
6. What will be the deliverable of the review?

For example, taking the review to be undertaken of the food manufacturers' delivery processes the answers to the questions above might be:
1. The ultimate clients are supermarket managers.
2. They need to receive goods at the specified delivery time, in perfect condition, 100 per cent of the time.
3. Currently only 90 per cent of deliveries are made at the specified time and 80 per cent are in perfect condition.
4. The opportunity is to improve both the timing and quality of delivery.
5. The customer will benefit as a result of the review from 100 per cent reliability and consistency.
6. The review should provide a more efficient and effective way of making deliveries on time plus a means of ensuring the total quality of delivered goods.

Identifying scope and size of the review

The project team also needs to formulate a preliminary picture of the scope of the review: who and what will be affected by the review and when. Also, they need to identify the degree of impact of the review. For example, in the case of the food manufacturer, should the review be restricted to one factory or several? Should it involve only transport and warehouse or manufacturing processes? It is only when the team have discussed and agreed on these points that they can decide what action needs to be taken and when.

Develop a work plan schedule for the review

Once the objectives for the review have been agreed by the project team, the team should set a timetable for the review including a meeting schedule. It is essential that all members of the project team understand the four stages of a process review and are familiar with the techniques involved in each. Often a half- to one-day training session outlining the different stages and the methodologies can be beneficial.

A work plan outline not only sets out the timeframe for the project but also itemizes the main segments of work and the information to be gathered. This can then be discussed with the sponsor. Constraints can also be agreed in terms of time, money and effort. In this way milestones can be set for the review and performance indicators agreed.

The work plan outline will usually contain a list of the most important elements of the process which need to be observed together with a proposed interview list. The project team may have to contact various sources to identify where it is best to gain information. (An organizational chart helps here.)

Work plan schedule

Once the elements of the work plan have been agreed they should be documented as a work plan schedule so that all project team members have a clear understanding of resources and time required. This can take a number of forms:
- Work action plan;
- GANTT charts;
- PERT chart.

Work action plans
These plans set out the stages of the activities in the review, what

Work Action Plan				
Project name:				Date:
Main activity number	Description of steps in activity	Responsibility	Timing	Desired outcome

Figure 6.7 Example of an uncompleted work action plan

will happen in each stage, when and who will be responsible. Figure 6.7 is an example of an uncompleted form.

GANTT charts

There are a number of computer spreadsheets which provide a means of displaying work schedules over time. Alternatively, handwritten charts can set out the planning sequence of work and resources needed.

GANTT charts are a method of displaying the work in a graphic format for a particular time period. Here tasks are displayed in the left-hand vertical column, time is displayed in the top horizontal row. Tasks are shaded to correspond with the estimated time for completion. (See Figure 6.8.)

PERT charts

A PERT chart is another method of graphically representing the workflow of a review. It shows the work sequence from start to finish of the project and the steps needed to be undertaken as part of each task in the review, together with a timescale. Figure 6.9 shows a typical PERT chart.

To begin a PERT chart ask the project team to brainstorm the activities involved in the review. It is helpful to write these out on sticky-backed (such as 'Post-it') notes so that they can then be reorganized into a sequence of activities.

Project name:				Date:				
Task No. w/c		20/2	27/2	6/3	13/3	20/3	27/3	3/4 10/4
1. Interview staff	——							
2. Document process			——					
3. Send questionnaires to customers					————			
4. Analyse results								——

Figure 6.8 Example of part-completed GANTT chart

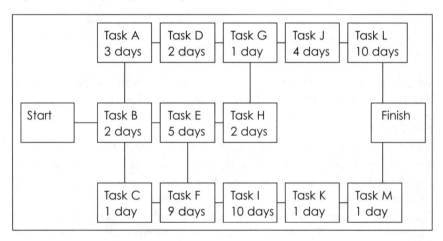

Figure 6.9 Example of a PERT chart

Once the activities have been brainstormed, the team can work out the critical path for the project. This is the longest path through the PERT chart. In the example above this is tasks C, F, E, H, G, J and L. These tasks are critical. If any delays occur in this sequence of activities the project timescale will be in jeopardy.

Many software packages, such as Microsoft Project, provide a quick means of working out critical paths, anticipated completion dates, etc. These are particularly helpful time-savers when there are delays or further unforeseen activities to be added to the project and the PERT chart needs to be reworked.

▪ Summary

- This chapter sets out the stages of initiating the review project.
- It emphasizes the need to gain commitment from senior management, one of whom, ideally, should sponsor the project.
- It explains how to form a project team and the need to understand team dynamics.
- It sets out techniques for identifying processes in need of improvement including diagnostic check-list, importance matrix and rating system.
- It details project management tools to help set objectives, to identify the customer and potential benefits of the review and to identify the scope and size of the review.
- Finally, it recommends that the team develop a work plan schedule using tools such as a work action plan, GANTT and PERT charts.

CHAPTER

7

STAGE 2: ASSESSMENT AND ANALYSIS

The purpose of stage 2 of the review is to allow the project team to familiarize themselves with the process in detail, to establish what are the gaps in the existing process and to determine how, ideally, it should be.

 ## Documenting the issues

When the project team first meets to assess the process, each team member will have differing perceptions/experience of the issues involved. Each member will also probably have an opinion on how best to gather information about the process. A useful first task for the project team, therefore, is to group their issues/opinions and record them. This can be used as the starting-point for discussion.

There are two methods which can be used to identify quickly issues. These are fishbone diagrams and cause and consequence diagrams.

Fishbone diagrams

The fishbone diagram was invented by the Japanese quality guru, Professor Ishigawa. It is a useful means of showing every element in an issue/problem and its interconnections, its causes and effects. Figure 7.1 is an illustration of some possible causes of poor deliveries, taking up our earlier example of the food

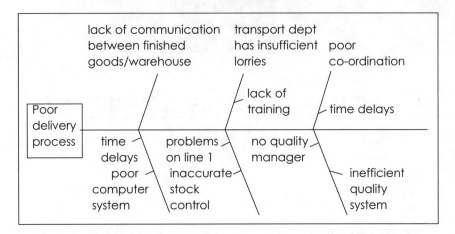

Figure 7.1 Example of a fishbone diagram for poor delivery process

manufacturing company. As can be seen from the example, the 'head' of the fish contains the problems or issues – the process to be reviewed. The fish has a backbone. Connected to the backbone are smaller bones which branch out to show the causes of the problems involved with the process. These branches or bones can each contain sub-branches/bones which cluster round a central cause.

The best way to use this methodology in a participative manner is for the project leader to draw a fish (head and backbone) on a flipchart paper placed in the centre of a table. All team members are given a marker pen rather than one person acting as 'scribe'. Everyone works together to add some bones to the backbone by jotting down issues. In this way all team members have an opportunity to record the issues as they see them.

Once the fish has been completed the project leader can ask the team to stand back and look at the drawing. By examining the words on each branch the team will probably discover recurring themes or duplication of issues. Likewise it is sometimes possible to immediately identify that there is one area of the process which causes more problems than others. In the example (Figure 7.1) the transport department appears to give more concern to participants than other potential causes of the inefficient process.

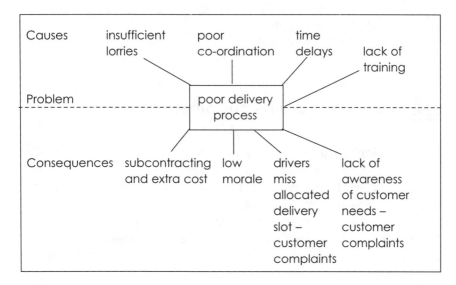

Figure 7.2 Example of a cause-and-consequence diagram for poor delivery process

Cause and consequence diagrams

A further means of documenting issues at this early stage is to use cause and consequence diagrams. Like fishbone diagrams, these diagrams allow project team members to map out their initial impressions on the possible causes of problems in the existing process and their probable consequences.

Figure 7.2 is an example of a problem participants saw in the delivery process which is now illustrated using the cause-and-consequence diagram. The process problem is shown in the centre of the diagram. Radiating from the top of the problem are probable causes and leading from it their probable consequences.

 Understanding the elements of the process

After recording the issues the team will now be ready for a fuller understanding of the process. There are three means by which to become more aware of the elements in the process.
1. Consultation with the customers of the process.
2. Consultation with people involved in the process –

employees and suppliers.
3.   Independent observation.

 ## Consultation with customers

Consultation with customers is a key part of the assessment stage as all processes should be customer driven. As the objective of the process therefore should be to satisfy the customer, the first stage in any review must be to discover:
1.   What the customer expects from the process.
2.   How satisfied the customer is with the process.
3.   What the customers believe should be done to improve the process.
The types of questions the project team needs to ask, therefore, are:
–   Who are the customers of the process – both external and internal customers?
–   What are the current requirements of customers?
–   How will these change in the future?
–   How satisfied are customers with the current outcome of the process?
–   What are the key elements of the process which are important to the customer?
–   What are potential areas for improvement?
–   What are the current strengths of the process so these can be built on?
–   What is best practice among the industry/other areas of comparison?
–   How customer-minded does the customer see the organization?
These general questions should result in the project team gaining an awareness of the strengths and weaknesses of the process deliverables in the eyes of the customer.

If a project team were undertaking a review of the delivery process which was used as an example earlier, they could gain information on customer satisfaction with the process as well as their expectations. In this instance it may prove useful to investigate also how customer expectations are formed. This will probably be through the customers' experience or perception of the performance of other delivery processes, not necessarily within the same industry but those which the customer considers best practice. The project team will probably also discover that the customer has a set of minimum standards to which he or she expects the manufacturer to perform.

In obtaining information from customers it is best to operate on a first-hand basis rather than relying on the views of sales people or intermediaries. Where possible the project team will have a better understanding if they can interview customers on a face-to-face basis, or at least experience their opinions at first hand. (For example, it may be feasible to run a series of focus groups where small numbers of customers meet to discuss service levels. However, in some industries where competition between customers is rife, this may not be feasible.)

Interview tips

The best means of gathering information from customers is through questions and answers provided during brief structured conversations. Not only is this a quick way of understanding the basic details of a situation, it also gives the project team members a feel for some of the intangible aspects of the process and what clients really require.

Interview preparation

Project team members need to pinpoint the issues and the questions to be discussed with customers and to prepare an outline agenda. This is particularly important when a number of customers are being interviewed as it provides the project team with a framework for analysis once the interviews have taken place.

When conducting interviews with customers, always establish the purpose of the meeting and how the information will be used. Clarify also whether the customer is making their comments on or off the record and hence how the meeting should be documented.

Good interviewers use a variety of open and closed questions to obtain the maximum information. Open questions such as who, what, where, why, how, when and 'tell me about' can allow the interviewee to expand on his or her opinions. Closed questions which elicit only one response are useful to clarify vagueness and to help summarize the interviewer's understanding.

It is useful to involve all team members in interviews with customers. Ideally two team members should attend each meeting. This allows two sets of impressions to be generated. Also questioning and recording responses can be difficult, therefore one of the pair of interviewers can question while the other listens and notes responses.

Meetings with customers should be scheduled to allow enough time to absorb and use the information obtained from the interview and to compare notes with the project team partner.

Tips on focus groups

Customer focus groups are another means of generating useful feedback. Here, groups of up to ten customers meet to discuss their impressions of the service provided and their expectations and satisfaction levels.

Guiding the discussion is a skilled task and often requires the use of a trained facilitator. Normally such sessions last between one and two hours and can be held on the process owner's premises or at a neutral venue. Both focus groups and interviews have the advantage of sending a powerful message to customers that the organization is interested in seeking their views. However, both mechanisms have a potential pitfall in that the customers may expect that action will be taken immediately as a result of the feedback they give. It is precautionary, therefore, to ensure that customers too understand the steps in the review process.

Tips on questionnaires

Once a qualitative feel has been obtained from customers the review team may wish to quantify this by the use of questionnaires. The disadvantage of sending questionnaires without first gaining feedback from customers directly on a face-to-face basis is that they do not allow a complete representation of customers' viewpoints to be canvassed. However, the advantage is that they are a speedy mechanism for obtaining wide-scale feedback.

Unfortunately, unless the benefit of completing a questionnaire is made clear to the customer, including what will be done with the information they are to provide, completion rates can be low. To overcome this problem effective questionnaires:

- are easy to complete;
- are laid out in a logical sequence and grouped by subject matter so that they are easy to follow;
- have a design which has impact and are simple in layout;
- keep questions short to allow speed of completion while allowing room for additional comments which the customer may wish to make;
- make return easy by ensuring there is a Freepost address or a means of quickly returning the questionnaire.

There is a danger that questionnaires may seem impersonal so they need to be accompanied by a request for information which is as friendly as possible. Preferably this should come from someone senior in the organization. Likewise, customers may require assurance that their comments will be treated in confidence.

Questionnaires should be constructed using a range of pre-determined responses for the customer. Sometimes these can be very simple such as Yes, No or Don't know, where the customer ticks the appropriate box corresponding to his or her opinion. However, it also helps to gauge the degree of customer opinions using scalar questions. Here customers are given a range of pre-determined responses, for example on a scale of 1 to 5 where 1 equals very poor and 5 equals very good, or a scale of responses such as 'very poor', 'poor', 'neither good nor poor', 'fairly good', 'very good'. In this way the team can evaluate the degree of satisfaction or dissatisfaction with the service and make comparisons between different elements of the process.

Figure 7.3 is an example of a customer service survey using the format described above.

Questionnaires can also be used to get a better understanding of customer expectations. This is achieved by including in the questionnaire mechanisms to canvas customers' level of satisfaction and also the importance factors of particular aspects of the service.

Customer Service Survey
We need to know how you rate our service so that we make it the best.

Dear Customer,

Help us to help you. Would you be kind enough to complete this questionnaire? It is an important part of a review which we are undertaking to monitor and improve the service we offer our customers. In particular we are keen to assess the level of service you received from our Customer Service Department in the last few weeks. Please note that this is a genuine research survey and your answers will be treated in the strictest confidence. Thank you in anticipation.

Yours faithfully

Peter Jones
General Manager

How would you rate our service in the following areas?

	Excellent	Good	Fair	Poor	N/A
Speed of response in reacting to your needs	☐	☐	☐	☐	☐
Accuracy of our understanding of your requirements	☐	☐	☐	☐	☐
Level of competence shown	☐	☐	☐	☐	☐
Fulfilment of promises made to carry out action	☐	☐	☐	☐	☐
Effectiveness of the action taken	☐	☐	☐	☐	☐
Clarity of any letters received from us	☐	☐	☐	☐	☐
Tone of any letters received from us	☐	☐	☐	☐	☐
Ease with which you were able to contact the department	☐	☐	☐	☐	☐
Level of courtesy shown by staff	☐	☐	☐	☐	☐
Overall, how would you rate our handling of your request?	☐	☐	☐	☐	☐

If you have any other comments please use the space below

Customer details:

Surname   Title   Initials
Company
Position
Address
Postcode

Thank you for taking the time to complete this questionnaire. Please seal it and send it in the envelope provided to the Freepost address. No stamp is required.

Figure 7.3 Example of a customer service survey

Quite often the assumption is made that the areas which have been highlighted as those of least satisfaction to customers should be the ones to address first in the process review. However, as the following satisfaction versus importance indicator demonstrates (Figure 7.4), when customers are asked to rate the importance of a given aspect of a service as well as to rate the company's performance, a further set of data can be obtained which shows the gap between expectations and performance. Now a new set of priorities emerges. Some of the aspects of the process which cause the customer most dissatisfaction are low on their list of priorities whereas others with which they are more satisfied in terms of performance rank higher in the list of importance.

In Figure 7.4 speed of telephone answering is more important to customers than clarity of product literature.

Gaining information from the process owners

Having obtained information from customers, the users and beneficiaries of the process, the project team needs to turn its attention to the views of the people involved in the process – 'the process owners'.

Prior to meeting with the process owners it is useful to collect general background information using organizational charts,

Service aspect	Performance %	Importance %	Gap
Speed of telephone answering	47	66	−19
Quality of product	61	71	−10
Clarity of product literature	53	23	+30

Figure 7.4 Performance versus importance analysis

general area overviews and any other relevant information so that the team gains some background knowledge of the process.

A meeting with the people in charge of the areas of the activities covered in the process should result in an understanding of the function performed in each area. This will help the team gain an overview of the overall process, recent and planned changes in systems or procedures and any other issues. As a result of this initial interview the project team should understand the process issues as seen from the management perspective, who is responsible for each activity and who should be involved in further interviews.

The next stage of interviews is with members of staff. These people can offer invaluable assistance in helping draw preliminary high-level flowcharts of the various activities in the process. Members of staff can also provide information on who does what within the function, plus a preliminary list of the functions/tasks showing work distribution.

Talking to staff will also increase the team's understanding of current practices and processes and gain interviewees' perceptions on issues. Process owners may also readily identify potential areas for improvements which may help overcome current problems. The more involvement members of staff and management have at this stage of the process the greater their understanding will be of the objectives of the review.

Direct observations

Interviews with process owners are a necessary part of the review. These should be supplemented with direct observation to obtain a detailed, more hands-on assessment of the process. Direct observation is one of the most useful ways of gathering information. However, this can be time-consuming so preparation is very important.

When observing the process in action, where at all possible team members should be unobtrusive. It is an acknowledged fact that behaviour changes under observation.

The outcome of observing procedures should be a detailed flowchart of the process and an overview of the systems used and outputs of the systems (for example, reports, etc.) Also, observation will help clarify which are the people who come into contact with each part of the process. (Remember again to elicit their comments on the potential improvement involved in each step of the process.)

Look out for procedures that do not add value to the customer or systems that don't seem to make sense. Other areas worth observing are manual procedures which could be automated and areas of consistent problems or complaints.

The underlying principles of observation are to involve staff, watch, ask questions, take notes. Do so by arranging a time period for observation which is relevant to process owners and not a hindrance.

Consult suppliers

Observation of the process will indicate which activities involve suppliers either from other parts of the organization or external to the organization. In addition to consulting with the process owners, suppliers can provide useful information by divulging their perceptions of the strengths and weaknesses of the activities in which they are involved.

Information can be obtained from suppliers on a one-to-one basis; or it may be possible to hold supplier focus groups where a number of complementary and non-competitive suppliers can share their experiences of being involved in the process. Again, suppliers' opinions on potential areas for improvement can prove invaluable.

Data collection tools

There are a number of analytical tools and techniques which are available to the project team to clarify the process in order to facilitate decision making. These tools are invaluable supplements to interviews and observations. They include:

Process flow diagrams

Following the initial assessment of the process which has been gained from interviews and observations, the project team should be in a position to prepare a hand-drawn representation of the process, laying out the steps and activities in sequential order. This serves a number of purposes:
–   It provides the project team with a greater understanding of the process flow.
–   It starts to identify areas of potential improvement through highlighting areas of problems or breakdowns.
There are a number of standard symbols which are used in process mapping:
⟶   Arrows are used to indicate the flow of work from one activity to the next.
▭   Rectangles represent activity steps.
◇   Decision points are represented by a diamond where yes and no decisions flow from the diamond points in differing directions according to the activities.
○   A circle represents the start of an activity.
▢   A rounded oblong, the end of the activity.
▱   A skewed rectangle information blockages.
Figure 7.5 is a process flow diagram for the delivery process of a computer supply company.
   Additional analytical information can be added to Figure 7.5:
–   Including the time taken at each activity step.
–   Highlighting the activities which add value to the customer.
–   Highlighting the interdependencies between the different parts of the activity sequences (these are normally colour-coded).
–   Calculating the effort at each stage of the activity sequence.
Similar analysis can be undertaken for information flows.

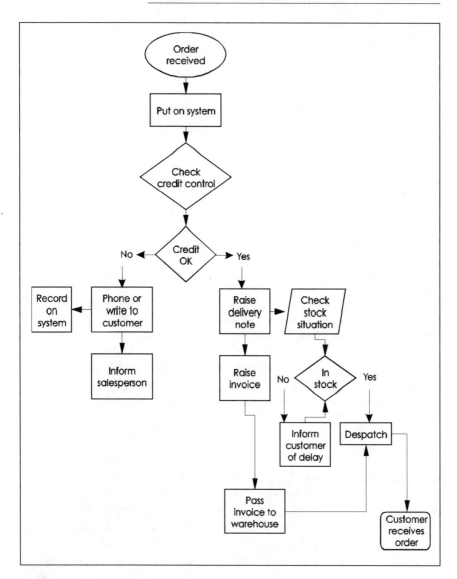

Figure 7.5 Example of a simple process flow diagram for the delivery process of a computer supply company

Information flow diagram

Information flow diagrams show the flow of information between different areas of the process in graphic format. This will help the team understand and clarify the information flow as well as

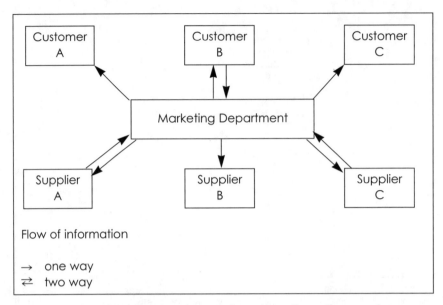

Figure 7.6 Simple example of an information flow diagram between a marketing department and its customers and suppliers

highlighting inefficient areas where there are information blockages. The project team can use this technique to identify missing information as well as information available.

Check-sheets

Check-sheets provide the project team with a mechanism for quantifying the number of incorrect areas of activities which occur in areas of blockages. For example, in the illustration in Figure 7.5, checking the stock situation is the activity which involves the most time and is the area which creates the most barriers of information. Staff in this area can therefore be encouraged to record on a regular basis the types of errors which occur. The information gathered helps detect patterns in a problem and how often certain events occur. Figure 7.7 is an example of a check sheet.

Problem logs

A problem log is a data collection tool which can be used to quantify the types and causes of problems. It is helpful in

Error	Day				
	1	2	3	4	5
Faulty printer	II	⧍⧍	III	I	I
Incorrect information	I	II	I	II	I
No availability	IIII	II	⧍⧍ II	II	III

Figure 7.7 Example of a part-completed check-sheet

identifying issues which may not previously have been noticed as part of the review. It also provides factual data as a basis for recommendations. The problem log usually involves manual completion of a form which sets out different types of problems and when they occur. To prepare the log project team members need to agree a representative time-period with the process owners. For ease of completion the types of problems already encountered can be listed so that these can be coded on the form. Allow for additional problems/issues which might arise by leaving space on the form.

Once staff have been briefed, forms should be completed on a daily basis. These should also be reviewed daily to ensure that there are no problems occurring from the way that the forms are laid out.

Figure 7.8 is an example of a problem log.

Work distribution log

The project team may find it helpful to quantify the effort expended on completing individual tasks in the process, or for example to determine an average daily working pattern. Work distribution logs are a further data collection tool. Here process owners keep a manual log of time spent on tasks over a representative period. Again, the time period needs to be agreed so as to avoid busy or slack times or periods that are untypical of the activity.

Problem log

Please complete as follows:

1. Enter the time you initially began working on/addressed the problem. Enter the time you resolved or discontinued working on the problem.
2. Enter the type of problem.
3. Enter the cause of the problem.
4. Record any comments that may clarify the problem further.

Time start	Time completed	Type of problem	Cause	Comments

Figure 7.8 Example of a problem log

During the period in which the forms are being completed project team members should check them periodically to ensure there are no problems in completion.

The tasks to be measured should be fairly clear after the interview and observation stage.

Sometimes problems occur when work distribution logs require too much detail, making it difficult for staff to fill out the logs, or alternatively the length of time it takes to complete the log may be prohibitive owing to the need to count activities manually.

A further problem may be that the terminology used on the work distribution log may not be clear to the people who will complete the log. To avoid this, use the same wording as that used within the department or area.

Furthermore, you should estimate the amount of data which is needed, as completion of work distribution logs are potentially

Customer Services Work Distribution Log			
Name:		Date:	
Code for activity	Time started	Time finished	Comments

Figure 7.9 Example of work distribution log

disruptive to staff. Be clear exactly what you will do with the data before you issue the logs to ensure that the information obtained will be relevant. Figure 7.9 is an example of a work distribution log.

The way the data is analysed when the logs have been collected will largely depend on the specific objectives of the review. You will probably need to do a number of different analyses on the data. Do not take anything at face value. Work distribution logs often cause project team members to raise other issues or questions with the process owners to gain a better understanding of what really happens in the activity sequence. Try to convert the raw data into graphic format by use of bar charts or pie charts or other instruments as applicable. This makes the analysis much easier to digest.

Many companies in the car industry have adopted work distribution techniques as part of process thinking as a means to ensure corporate survival. Rolls-Royce is an example. It used the technique to improve quality and productivity by concentrating on its core processes and outsourcing accessory parts.

Pareto diagrams

Once data have been converted to graphs look for potential correlations between two factors. For example, Pareto, an Italian economist, discovered there was often a correlation in the order of 80/20 (this can be 70/30 or even 60/40) between two variables. He based this concept on his studies of the Italian economy where he found that 80 per cent of the wealth of the country was owned by 20 per cent of the people.

The same principles can be applied to issues surrounding process inefficiency or blockages. Often it can be found, for example, that 70 or 80 per cent of the causes of problems in processes originate from 20 per cent of the activities.

To establish this a bar graph is usually drawn identifying the important elements of the activity using percentage measurements. Figure 7.10 is an example of a Pareto chart which shows that the most frequent cause of complaint is not the most expensive one to solve.

Other hard analysis

Other measures to help in the analysis which is being conducted by the project team involve quantifying different ratios of performance. These can include sales or profitability per employee, employee turnover, employee absenteeism, output per manufacturing line, etc. The variables will depend on the process itself.

DHL have developed a system of activity-based costing to support its business reengineering programme. In the mid-1980s DHL knew a lot about the performance of its business; what it did not know was the cost of its product, the cost of its customers, the profitability of its customers by product, customer retention, etc. In 1990 an attempt was made to introduce a costing system to support the business. This met with little success. In 1992 DHL developed a second-generation activity-based costing system to support its process reengineering initiative. It used the cost management study to identify opportunities to reduce cost or deploy resources more effectively. The system helps DHL compare value costs and service standards of outputs.

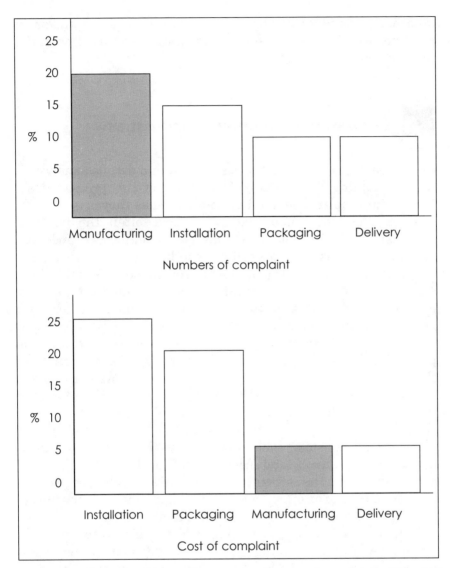

Figure 7.10 Example of Pareto charts comparing type of complaint with cost of complaint

 ## Analysis of existing reports

The project team probably will also find that the area they are investigating produces a sequence of reports or data on how it currently operates. It is worthwhile therefore reviewing this information to identify what further data is required and/or, in addition, whether the current reports indicate areas of potential problems or weaknesses.

 ## Documenting problems and issues

As the team is conducting the assessment and detailed analysis it will be gaining invaluable information on the process itself. Issues and problems should be documented as they arise.

Team members should be aware that often the outward manifestation of a problem/issue merely camouflages deeper root causes. Problems or issues can be seen like an onion with many layers of skin. An initial symptom or problem such as staff taking a great deal of time to enter information on the computer may hide a deeper issue such as duplication of effort – where two parallel systems, one manual and one computerized, may exist. This in turn may camouflage the real issue or problem with the process in that staff may not be fully trained or confident in using the computer. Alternatively the computer-based system may not be the most appropriate. As the review progresses, therefore, the project team will find it beneficial to record issues.

In documenting issues surrounding the process, the project team should consider such problems as duplication of effort, unnecessary controls and poor communication. As discussed earlier, it is often the soft cultural issues which influence people's performance and project team members should be particularly observant of process owners' attitudes and behaviour.

It helps to sort problems into logical order and present them in a readable format, outlining next steps to be taken as the review progresses. A part-completed issues list of one organization is shown in Figure 7.11.

 ## Reviewing data and producing a gap analysis

Once the project team decide that they have gathered sufficient data to be able to understand fully the process, a gap analysis can

Issue	Description	Next step
1. Delays in information from warehouse	30% complaints due to delay in information	Investigate computer stock system Instigate relationship between credit control and warehouse

Figure 7.11 Example of a part-completed issues list

Customer requirement	Current performance
– 100% product reliability	– 85% product reliability
– 24-hour helpline	– 7.5-hour helpline
– individual account management	– team account management
– JIT supplies	– 14-day supply call off

Figure 7.12 Example of a part-completed gap analysis

be produced. A gap analysis is a means of assessing what needs to be done in the current process to bring about improvement. It sets out potential areas for change; it draws comparisons between the current situation and customer requirements; and it draws on knowledge of 'best practice'. An example of a part-completed gap analysis is shown in Figure 7.12.

In this way the project team have a framework for reviewing the current process. The next step, as we will see in the following chapter, is to identify not only the gap in performance but how this gap can be closed.

 Review of progress to date

There is also an opportunity at this stage of the review for the project team members to review their progress and how they work together as a team. For example, has everyone taken responsibility for action? Is the timescale set out at the beginning of the review still realistic? How well is the team using project management tools? Is everyone clear about their role? Is there duplication of effort? What barriers, if any, has the team had to overcome? What has been the reaction of the process owners to the review? How much has the review cost to date?

Assessing these and other such questions may help the team to identify possible routes forward when it comes to the implementation of recommendations.

 ## Assessment review

Whatever method is used to undertake a detailed analysis of the current process, the project team will find it necessary to record the outcome in order to clarify their findings. They will also probably need to present the outcome of this study to their sponsor so that problems and issues of the current process can be evaluated in terms of their importance and next steps agreed.

Prepare a discussion document for the meeting with the sponsor. This document can outline the team's findings with regard to the current process and discuss the results of the gap analysis. It can also detail the issues/problems inherent in the current process and organize these into categories, thus beginning to prioritize major and minor problems. A typical assessment document will contain the following headings.

1. Current status of review.
2. Overview of findings of assessment and detailed analysis of process.
3. Customer requirements and expectations.
4. Gap analysis.
5. Major problems/issues with current process.
6. Secondary issues.
7. Proposed next steps.

Once a meeting is held with the sponsor it may be necessary to verify some details of the initial findings before the next phase can begin.

 ## Balance of views

The project team who undertake the assessment and detailed

analysis of the review process often find that this stage can be difficult because of the need to go into great depth to gain an understanding of the process while at the same time maintaining an objective overview of client needs. However, the importance of careful assessment can be seen in the results of a number of organizations' process thinking.

For example, in 1990 Ericsson, the telecommunications company, identified several general and specific processes common to the whole group. These were documented within each of the local main companies.

A systematic methodology for business process management was introduced to the company. Its first stage was the identification of processes. At a workshop attended by 50 managers from across the business, critical processes were pinpointed as marketing, sales, order supply, product planning, product provisioning and customer support. Processes and teams were appointed to establish reviews of the core processes. Data was collected and analysed. This was subsequently used to supervise, control and improve business activity. Results included the reduction of time to market new products from 17.5 months to 7.5 months.

Having a documented operations system that describes all the company's processes and activities gives Ericsson a common view of how work is performed throughout the company. It serves as the starting-point for improvements. The planning and detailed analysis phases of the review are updated as improvements are achieved.

 ## Summary

- This chapter explains the steps in the assessment and detailed analysis phase of the review.
- It sets out techniques which can be used to document issues/problems in the current process. These include fishbone diagrams, cause and consequence diagrams together with interviews, questionnaires and observations.
- Data collection tools such as process flow diagrams, information flow diagrams, check-sheets, problem logs,

work distribution logs and Pareto diagrams are explained.
- The final part of the chapter deals with reviewing the data and producing a gap analysis.
- At this stage in the study the project team should present their preliminary findings to the sponsor as well as reviewing their team performance to date.

CHAPTER

8

STAGE 3: DESIGNING PROCESSES

The next stage in the process review involves two steps. First, looking from the outside in – or 'thinking out of the box'. This describes the technique of imagining the Utopian scenario which best meets customer requirements and then working backwards to identify what needs to change in the current process to bring it up to its ideal form. The second phase of this stage involves developing an ideal solution.

 Redesign tools

This chapter describes four techniques which can be used to design an improved process. These are:
1. brainstorming;
2. greenfield design;
3. benchmarking;
4. best practice analysis.
Underlining these techniques is the need to challenge basic assumptions about the current process. The 'why, why, why?' technique may be useful here. Often people cannot remember why existing processes are set up the way they are. Assumptions are made about what the customer wants, why the process is configured in its current manner, who does what, where the activities take place, when the activities take place, what resources are required and how work is allocated. By asking questions such as:

- Why does the customer need the output in this way?
- Why are the activities undertaken in this sequence?
- Why are resources required from outside the department or area?
- Why is the work allocated in this sequence?

Project team members can hit out at some of the underlying premises on which the current processes are built.

Brainstorming techniques

Brainstorming is a useful tool to generate new ideas. When it comes to inventing a new idea there are three potential sources:
1. You can invent it within the team.
2. You can copy other people's ideas which have been successful.
3. You can bring in technology which incorporates the idea into the process (technology frequently enables organizations to break old assumptions).

When brainstorming is done in the correct fashion it allows team members to 'freewheel' so that they can come up with potential solutions. There are some general problems, however, associated with brainstorming as a technique. Sometimes the brainstorming process can be dominated by one or two people, either those with the loudest voices or the most ideas. The team can run out of ideas; ideas can be considered and rejected out of hand; team members can have their own 'ideal solutions' and close their minds to potential ideas from other parties.

The most effective brainstorming sessions take place out of the work environment and are led by a trained facilitator who ensures that everyone has their say. It is important that ideas are evaluated at a separate session.

There are several novel techniques which can be used to encourage everyone to participate and to be creative in their thinking.

Individual lists

Brainstorming sessions should begin by allowing everyone to gather their thoughts. Before a session opens give project team members time to each write down their ideal solutions or possible solutions, then ask individuals to share their ideas with the rest of the team. This allows quieter members of the team an opportunity to put their ideas forward. All ideas should be recorded on a flip-chart. Where brainstorming sessions go wrong it is often because ideas are 'screened' by the person writing the ideas on the flip-chart. This person may decide not to add to the list ideas which seem impractical!

Consequences

Another means of gaining everybody's views and also building on the ideas of other people is to adopt the route of consequences. This technique is similar to the childhood game. Everyone in the team has a piece of paper, they each write down an idea and pass the paper on to the person sitting next to them. This person then looks at the idea which has been written on the paper and writes a complementary idea, building on what has been written. Alternatively, if they cannot build on this idea, they write down a new idea before passing on the paper to the person sitting next to them.

Forced associations

If the team runs out of ideas a novel way of trying to generate additional ideas is to use the technique of forced associations. This method involves the team making 'creative leaps'. The team needs to first generate a list of words which have nothing to do with the process. For example, here is a list which was generated at random.

- planes;
- lamp;
- telephone;
- warmth;
- questionnaire;
- paper-clip.

Team members write the words on pieces of paper or on a flip-chart. The concept is that the team then use these words to force an association between the word on the paper or flip-chart and the ideal solution. For example, if the team were trying to generate ideas to improve the order-to-delivery process of one service company, here are some forced associations between the list of words and ideal solutions to the current problems:

Planes	=	give senior managers an overview of the difficulties.
Lamp	=	lighten the workload – sub-contract.
Telephone	=	change to telephone-based not paper-based system.
Questionnaire	=	gain feedback from customers on a regular basis.
Paper clip	=	link activities together.

Ideas checklist

A further mechanism is an ideas check-list. This involves working through a series of questions such as:
- What is the ideal solution to the problem?
- What is the situation now?
- What will have to change?
- What is stopping the changes taking place now?
- What action is to take place first?
  etc.

An alternative check-list is to ask:
- What would happen if the steps in the process were reordered?
- What would happen if work was reallocated to other departments/areas or outsourced?
- What would happen if the customer took on part of the work?
- What would happen if the number of interfaces in the process were reduced?
- Can centralization take place? Or decentralization?
- Can a variety of tasks be combined into one role?
- Can activities be spread out so they are performed by several groups?
- Is it possible to make decisions as early as possible in the process or to push decision making back?
- Is it possible to standardize parts of the process?
- Is it possible to improve service levels?
- Is it possible to increase precision?
- How can more value be added to the process?

During the brainstorming sessions responses should be encouraged but the project team should not discuss the detail at this point; rather, original or bizarre ideas should be welcomed.

Towards the end of the brainstorming session ideas need to be organized so that those which are related can be grouped together. This will give the team a feel as to which ideas are most appealing to the group or which parts of the process give most concern.

At a separate session the benefits or disadvantages of each of the ideas can be discussed and a selection made of those which are considered to be the best. (The next chapter deals with methods for evaluating solutions.)

Greenfield design

A further technique which proves invaluable in redesigning the process flow is greenfield design. This technique enables creative new processes to be developed without being restricted by the current situation. It is also a means of encouraging creative thinking. The term originates from a building of new premises in an undeveloped location rather than trying to improve existing buildings. The idea is to completely innovate a process as if the current process does not exist. The new sequence of activities should exactly meet customer requirements and achieve radical improvements.

In essence the team is starting with a blank sheet of paper. Considering customer needs, the team can decide what inputs are required in the process and its critical features. Keeping the process as simple as possible, an ideal flow of activities can then be developed. Useful questions are:
1. What would the customer do if they were redesigning the process?
2. What is the simplest way to deliver the output?
As the team is plotting out the new process they should also document their thoughts behind each step. Also the team should critically evaluate the flow of the process activities to determine their feasibility.

The next step is to compare the ideal 'greenfield design' with the 'brownfield' or existing process. By making this comparison redundant steps in the current process can be identified.

The team then has a choice: do they opt for radical step change and reengineer the process; or redesign the process so that it better meets customer demands but the process still keeps many

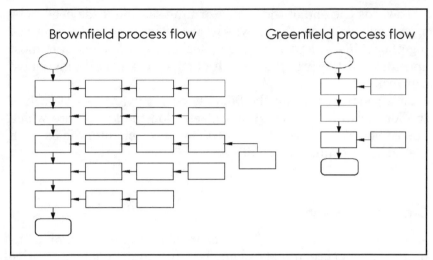

Figure 8.1 Example of a comparison between greenfield and brownfield processes

of the features of the current procedures; or should they merely make limited improvements to the existing processes?

There are many software packages available in the market-place which help model existing and potential processes. The software tools usually support process improvements, process redesign and process reengineering by providing such features as structural analysis, modelling and charting of processes, as well as simulation and animation facilities and workflow automation. The main advantage of computerized models are that they can be updated easily. They allow users to perform 'what if' modelling and view time and value analyses for each process.

Granada UK Rental, for example, have developed their own process software modelling tools. These were initially piloted. A software toolset has now been introduced across the company to develop process modelling and workflow charts.

Whether the process re-design is undertaken via computer or on a hand-drawn basis, it is invaluable to review the process flow with the sponsor and ultimate customers of the process to evaluate its feasibility.

Benchmarking

One of the problems often encountered when the project team decides to redesign the process is that the sponsor of the organization and the process owners may not believe that radical improvements need to be made or that they have the capability to undertake the changes. Benchmarking is a powerful method of identifying and understanding outstanding practices from within the same organization or from another organization to help improve performance. It is useful in helping overcome internal complacency and in stretching goals. In this sense it helps accelerate change.

Benchmarking is now an accepted tool for companies undertaking total quality initiatives. It forms part of the European Quality Award and, in the US, the Malcolm Baldridge Award. Companies such as British Airways, Rover, Xerox and Royal Mail have championed benchmarking in this country. It is now being used throughout many organizations.

Design to distribution (D2D), a subsidiary of computer systems group ICL, produces more than a million printed circuit-boards a year, making it Europe's fifth largest manufacturer of circuit-boards. D2D has moved from being an internal client supplier serving its parent company ICL to supplying external customers.

D2D uses advanced benchmarking practices to measure its processes internally against ICL corporate strategic quality models, with customers and suppliers, and against its competitors. Everyone in the company is trained in process management and improvements. Since 1987 the training has involved over 2,700 people. Critical processes are determined by management at an annual strategic review supported by quarterly updates and monthly business reviews. These processes are then benchmarked to help accelerate and manage change.

Stages of benchmarking

There are four stages in the benchmarking process.

The planning phase of benchmarking involves many of the detailed analysis and assessment techniques outlined in the previous chapter. It is important that the project team gain a full understanding of the process in order to be able to decide what elements it wishes to benchmark.

The second phase in a benchmarking study is to select benchmarking partners. These can be internal or external to the organization. Within the organization the project team needs to

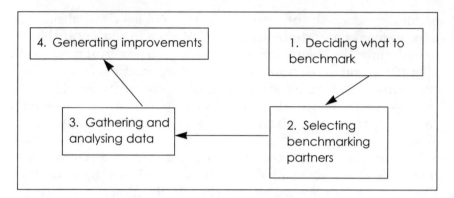

Figure 8.2 The four stages of benchmarking

identify units or areas undertaking similar activities. For example, many manufacturing companies benchmark their different manufacturing plants. They identify key performance criteria to establish measures and draw comparison between each of their operating units.

If the team needs to look outside the organization they can make contact with potential benchmarking partners, either directly or via benchmarking clearing houses whose purpose is to put organizations with similar processes in contact with each other. Information is normally exchanged with outside organizations on a confidential basis. Much data can be obtained from written reports, trade associations or articles, or just from over the phone. Benchmarking does not necessarily require lengthy visits to the other parts of the organization or external companies.

Phase three of benchmarking comprises data collection and analysis. Here the project team need to prepare and administer questions to gain information from benchmarking partners on a face-to-face basis, via the telephone or by questionnaires.

Project team members will probably need also to develop a database to tabulate responses and to make direct comparisons. Gather data both on hard performance measures and some of the 'soft' issues which support working practices. For example, an organization's revenue per employee ratio may be high yet this fact alone will not indicate to project team members the reasons for this performance. The reasons may be due to cultural factors such as employee motivation, career and development opportunities and internal communications. Alternatively, they may be caused by working practices or organizational structure.

Benchmarking partner analysis			
Company	A	B	C
Revenue per employee	15,960	23,000	19,120
No. of customers per employee	120	50	189
Advertising/sales ratio (%)	3	10	13

Figure 8.3 Example of benchmarking analysis

When analysing the performance and practice data, therefore, the team need to identify what are the enablers which bring about results. In this way it is possible to identify not only gaps in performance between the process which the project team are studying and benchmarking partners but also what differences there are in working style and methodology.

The final stage of the benchmarking study is generating solutions. This means establishing short-term and long-term improvement goals. We discuss evaluation and implementation techniques in the next chapter.

Best practice benchmarking

One variation of benchmarking which brings about step change is to identify best practices. This is a tool which can be used for comparing processes to those which are considered the best in class. Organizations such as Rank Xerox have developed this methodology in order to create a competitive edge. They looked at organizations which were considered to be best in class in order to identify how they achieved their levels of performance. Rank Xerox were among the first organizations to champion best practice benchmarking during the 1980s. Subsequently, organizations such as Royal Mail and British Airways have used this technique to improve existing processes by learning from the best of other, more effective processes.

The technique involves making a shortlist of companies who perform similar tasks and who are considered outstanding, and then studying their processes.

Best practice partners can be in similar industries or non-comparable industries. For example, an organization setting up a telephone customer service operation could look at other such operations in, for example, the field of airline reservations, car hire reservations, or other part of the service sector which are considered best in class. A comparison could then be made between each of the processes to see why and how they work.

Best practice is particularly helpful when charting an ideal process using the Greenfield design technique. By understanding what is the best it is possible to incorporate the practices of the best-of-class organizations into the newly designed process flow.

 ## Developing an ideal solution

The outcome of this stage of the project review should be the redesign of processes. The review team should check, for example, that they have identified added-value steps which can be developed in the current process, that redundant steps in the process have been removed and that steps are automated when possible. The overriding factor is that customer needs should be catered for in a better fashion in the new redesigned process. The result of this stage, therefore, should be:

1. agreement on the ideal for an improved process;
2. a summary of potential improvements supported by a process flowchart ;
3. recommendations on proposed solutions.

The team will find it beneficial to record their potential solutions. This normally takes the form of a written document which summarizes the options and provides a step-by-step illustration of procedures that meet customer requirements. The document will outline the detail of the potential new or changed processes, usually with reference to the current process.

 ## Whitbread Beer Company

Whitbread Beer Company is an example of an organization which has effectively utilized many of the techniques outlined in the review process so far. A division of Whitbread plc, the company was formed out of an internal reorganization in 1990 when three divisions were put together with the former corporate marketing function to form an integrated beer production, wholesaling and distribution business. This was felt by Whitbread to be a necessary move in response to the changes forced on the brewing industry in the wake of the investigation into it by the Monopolies and Mergers Commission.

By 1992 the recession in the UK was affecting the brewing industry and it was realized that the opportunities for volume growth were limited at that time and into the future. It was decided therefore that a 'step change' approach was required to identify a fast response to the market changes in terms of revenue generation and cost saving opportunities. After discussions with several management consultancy groups the concept of business process reengineering (BPR) was selected as the most appropriate tool. In addition, as the concept of BPR was deemed to be complex to explain generally at that stage, it was decided to position the project as the Business Effectiveness Review (BER).

A group of seven Beer Company senior managers were selected to form a team to carry out the BER initial stages. The team was designed to be cross-functional with representatives from finance, manufacturing, human resources, systems, marketing and sales strategy. All were senior managers reporting to board directors to ensure that the best people were used in the project.

The Beer Company board acted as the project steering group. The project was perceived in three phases:

> Phase 1 Review (the current position)
> Phase 2 Redesign (reengineering of the processes)
> Phase 3 Action (implementation of the changes)

Finally, external consultants were commissioned to provide consultancy support to the project. It was felt to be important to involve consultants in order to ensure a holistic approach to the project and to create a catalytic effect. Also, they were able to provide or suggest best practice knowledge and experiences to aid the process redesign phase.

The objectives of the BER were:
–   to understand and meet customer needs
–   to examine and re-engineer business processes

– to maintain business focus
– to co-ordinate existing improvement initiatives
while ensuring a balance between quality, service, cost and time.

The BER was taking place against a background of existing change and improvement activities within the business and all of these had to be co-ordinated within an overall framework. In parallel, a major project to replace the majority of business systems within the Beer Company was also underway and the two projects quickly became integrated.

Other relevant factors were the identification of the key customer channels of trade and major quality and service initiatives which were already in progress. During 1991 work had been carried out to separate out the different channels of trade among Beer Company customers, resulting in four internal business units being established in early 1992 to cover:
– take-home (the off-licence trade);
– independent free trade;
– multiples (external chains and other Whitbread divisions);
– other brewers and wholesalers.

Also, a major quality and service initiative had been launched and one-day awareness workshops had been held for all Beer Company personnel. This had evolved into more comprehensive two-day customer care courses for personnel involved in customer contact activities. In parallel, BS 5750 accreditation was underway for all of the industrial locations and functions.

The BER project team set about identifying the key business processes in the Beer Company so that they could be reengineered. This involved analysing the current position and determining the main issues. In turn, this allowed the drafting of proposals for new reengineered processes taking account of best practice. The impact of these changes in terms of organization, costs, people, training needs, etc. were assessed together with the potential benefits and implementation timescale.

The methodology for this review included:
– business appraisal and process map preparation;
– functional and process diagnostics;
– departmental activity analysis;
– customer needs analysis.

The first three of these tools were largely internal but the customer analysis focused on the external by asking customers about their perception of the Beer Company's efficiency, particularly in comparison with competitors. This work highlighted the difference between assumed knowledge of customer needs and the reality of the customer views. The results were mixed, some services assessed as good, some comparable with competitors and some in need of improvement. This allowed the process reengineering to concentrate on what adds value for the customer, bearing in mind:

–   the aspirations of customers relative to the practicability of providing enhanced service; and

–   similarly, the costs of enhanced service levels and the willingness of customers to pay either directly or indirectly.

It also highlighted the need for ongoing monitoring of customer needs and perceptions, and appropriate mechanisms have been developed. The review process identified the key business processes which would benefit from reengineering. These ranged from classical cross-functional activities such as order cycle management and new product development to more functionally contained processes such as manufacturing management and cellar service charging.

Phase 2 of the review consisted of cross-functional project teams building on the work of the Phase 1 team in a far more detailed review of each business process area, and validating or revising the initial proposals. At the end of Phase 2 in the spring of 1993 a complete review of Beer Company activities had been undertaken with proposals established and agreed to reengineer process areas across the business.[10]

 ## Summary

•   This chapter outlines the third phase in the review process which involves designing the ideal process.

•   An explanation is provided of different redesign tools including brainstorming, greenfield design, benchmarking and best practice benchmarking.

•   By the end of this phase of the study the team will have documented ideal solutions to meet customer requirements.

STAGE 4: IMPLEMENTATION

The final stage of the process review involves evaluating potential solutions and putting forward recommendations for changes to the process. Once recommendations have been agreed the team will finally have to agree the all-important implementation plan and how subsequent performance will be monitored and reviewed.

 ## Evaluating solutions

By the end of Stage 3 of the study, the review team will have identified a number of ideal solutions to the process. There are a number of techniques varying in degrees of sophistication which will facilitate a selection by the project team of the most appropriate outcome. These include three-star rating scenario analysis, cost–benefit analysis and strategic analysis.

Three-star rating

A simple and quick technique for getting a 'gut reaction' to the potential improvements that can be made to a process is to adopt the technique of three-star rating.

To do this alternative solutions are written on a flip-chart for all team members to see. Each team member is then allocated three stars. The stars are used to indicate his or her preference for the best solutions. Each team member can allocate the three stars either to three different ideas (three x one star each) or simply to one idea (where they allocate all three stars) alternatively to two ideas where they can allocate one and two stars respectively. Once each team member has allocated their stars the number of stars given to each solution is totalled. In this way a ranking of preferences can be obtained. This will give the project team a feel for the team's overall preference.

Scenario analysis

One means of ensuring that proposed solutions are robust enough to be valid in a changing environment is to adopt the tool of scenario analysis. This involves team members developing a set of scenarios, taking into account future market environments and internal systems and organizations. For example, a project team was considering redesigning a process. Its recommendations had highlighted several alternative solutions including introducing new technology, reorganizing responsibilities and bringing in new procedures. The team developed three alternative scenarios based on potential conditions that would be in place in the external environment in the future. They then discussed the opportunities each presented and made a comparison between the alternatives.

This form of scenario development is a particularly useful technique to simulate the effect of changes in processes. It has been used by a number of organizations including British Telecom. When British Telecom wished to reorganize their Directory Enquiries service they simulated the effect of networking 50 automatic distribution centres together so that they could ensure that any consequent changes could be undertaken with fewer risks.

ICI Acrylics used a 'reengineering laboratory' to provide a secure environment for the redesign team leading a pan-European project to build and test a prototype model of the reengineered business.

Cost–benefit analysis

An alternative and more traditional technique is to produce a cost–benefit analysis for each of the potential solutions. Here the

Activity	Cost A	Cost B	Cost C	Benefit A	Benefit B	Benefit C	Cost–Benefit ratio

Figure 9.1 Example of a cost–benefit matrix

cost of each solution in terms of time, people and money can be quantified against the potential benefits to stakeholders – shareholders, customers, employees and suppliers.

Cost–benefit analysis is normally undertaken by recording costs and benefits in a matrix format. Where possible, both costs and benefits are quantified so that an estimate can be made of their ratio. Where it is not possible to quantify 'soft' benefits, an indication of the scale of impact of the benefit can be made. Figure 9.1 is an example of a cost–benefit matrix.

Strategic fit/customer needs

A further form of analysis is to rank each potential solution in terms of how well it fits the strategy of the organization and how well it fulfils customers' needs. A strategic fit/customer needs matrix can be devised as outlined in the example where solutions which fall into the quadrant representing high strategic fit and high fulfilment of customer needs are those which appear most suitable. Figure 9.2 is an example of a strategic fit/customer need matrix.

Putting forward recommendations

The project team should now be at the stage where they can put forward recommendations to the board of the company or other senior management on how the process can be improved.

The project team will benefit from discussing their recommendations with the sponsor prior to making a full presentation to other senior managers. In this way the project team can discuss with the sponsor the likely reactions of the people who will be involved in making decisions at a senior level.

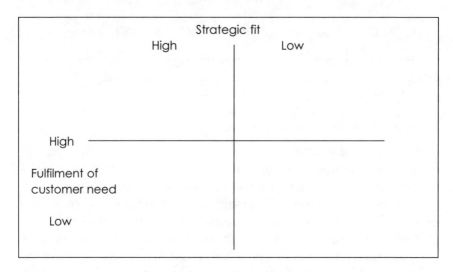

Figure 9.2 Example of a strategic fit/customer need matrix

When preparing recommendations a useful tip is to remember to identify short-term steps that can produce 'quick wins'.

Presenting the recommendations of the team

It is likely that only a few people from the project team will be required to present the findings of the study to senior executives from the company and to put forward the team's recommendations. It is therefore imperative that the people chosen from the team to present their case have good presentation skills – many projects fall at this hurdle because project team members are not effective in putting their views forward.

In presenting recommendations the team need to outline the background to the project and give a brief summary of the steps that have been taken during the review. Particular emphasis in the presentation should be given to customer requirements and the gap analysis which has been undertaken, together with the results in summary format of the detailed analysis and assessment.

The detailed analysis should help quantify potential benefits of the changes proposed. These benefits can be set out in terms of how the proposals better meet customer requirements as well as

Recommendations	Action required	Cost implications	Responsibility	Time-frame	Benefit

Figure 9.3 Example of an implementation action plan

the needs of other stakeholders such as shareholders and employees. The benefits which can be accentuated, for example, could include higher customer satisfaction and retention, better job security and higher job satisfaction for employees, greater teamwork and more opportunities for personal development. The review team will also need to quantify the cost involved of the improvements.

When the team presents their recommendations they should be prepared to present an overview of the situation rather than going into detail. A detailed analysis can be presented in written format to supplement the verbal presentation. Where senior managers need to digest a large amount of information it is often helpful to send out a summary of the report prior to the presentation of findings. In this way senior managers and decision makers can obtain an overview of the study and prepare questions to be asked at the presentation.

Project management techniques

As part of the presentation senior managers will expect to see proposals on the way forward – what should be the next steps. Project management techniques such as GANTT and PERT charts (see Chapter 6) can be used by the team to represent the stages of implementation of the proposals in graphic format. Action plans can be particularly helpful in setting out the sequence of activity needed to implement the proposed changes. These should show recommendations, action required, cost implications, responsibility, time-frame and benefit. An example is given in Figure 9.3.

Another tool is a milestone chart (see Figure 9.4). This plots the critical phases of the implementation of the recommendations.

Activity	Deliverable	Responsibility	Estimated timescale

Figure 9.4 Example of a milestone chart

In other words, what should be delivered at each stage and who will be responsible. This will ensure that the implementation team have a clear direction and signposts to which to adhere.

 ## Life of the project team

Once approval has been given to the team on how the current process can be improved, it is highly probable that the project team will need to reconsider its role and who are the best people to lead the implementation phase. It may not be appropriate, for example, for the team in its current format to undertake this task. Other steering groups or task groups may need to be formed to take the recommendations forward.

One organization set up smaller task groups led by members of the original steering group to lead the improvement activity. This had the advantage of creating a better understanding of the objectives of the review and sharing the learning of the original team with other people throughout the business.

If the original project team does disband they should not do so before sharing the learning points from the process to date, both among themselves and with others. Valuable lessons will have been learnt from the way the review members acted together as a team as well as their interaction with other people both inside and outside the organization.

Change management techniques

Once implementation task groups have been formed, be it new teams or the original project team, their first task will be to identify not only what needs to change to meet the agreed objectives but also how the changes will be made.

What to change

The task groups who are going to implement the improvements to existing processes will first need to familiarize themselves with the reasons for the proposed changes and, second, to consider how the changes will have impact on other parts of the organization and what therefore needs to change in turn.

For example, when one financial institution decided to introduce new working patterns to a department which had traditionally been paper bound, the changes involved not only introducing new technology but the development of staff-specific training together with changes in human resource policy to support the new working practices.

One way of taking an overview of the impact of the changes to take place is to consider the people issues, technologies, and structure (see Figure 9.5).

McKinsey's seven S's framework

Management consultants McKinsey have developed a framework for considering the impact of change on the organization. They recognize that change will often impact on strategy, structure, style, shared values, staff, skills and systems.

Strategy

Change takes place most effectively when people affected by the changes can understand its strategic relevance. The task groups leading the implementation process should be clear therefore on the strategic relevance of the improvements. These can be

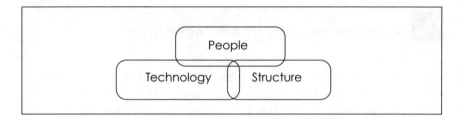

Figure 9.5 The impact of change

expressed in terms of strategic goals for the improved or new process. For example, the process may help the organization:

1. offer speedier, high-quality service to the customer, thereby increasing customer satisfaction;
2. improve employee motivation via the introduction of team working and performance-related pay;
3. provide opportunities for better partnerships with suppliers;
4. improve the return to shareholders.

Structure

Most process improvements facilitate simpler ways of working. This often involves delayering the organization so that the business benefits from flatter, more open, less formal structures. The task group should consider the best way for the process to be implemented in terms of its operational structure, both from the customers' point of view and that of the perspective of employees.

Later in the chapter we consider how best to communicate and involve employees in structural change. The task groups will also need to consider what training and development will need to take place to help bring about a smooth transition from one structure to another. For example, when one organization set up a new customer response centre, it trained not only front-line staff in new customer handling skills, it also developed training for its team leaders and managers in their new role.

Leadership style

A further question to consider is what style of leadership is required to support the new process. This is particularly important because if the preceding stages leading to the recommendations of improvement have gone well, the change period requires leadership and clarity of vision.

It is increasingly acknowledged that the role of the manager is changing within UK businesses. A recent survey by MORI aimed to explore what today's business leaders perceive as the nature and requirement of leadership and to identify the essential characteristics of good leadership. The research was conducted among 700 main board directors using a telephone questionnaire. Over 80 per cent of respondents saw a leader primarily as a motivator who has the ability to get others involved and stimulate their interest. Thirty per cent of respondents saw the leader as an innovator concerned with creating a new vision or new ideas. A further 32 per cent saw the role of leader as coach. Only 14 per cent described the leader as the 'boss', which is a traditional term associated with control.

The characteristics and attitudes which are therefore required of leaders around whom future business performance will revolve are strength of vision and the ability to motivate others to share that vision and ensure that the vision is carried out. Many blue-chip organizations are encouraging their executives to undergo leadership education and training to help those organizations turn their vision into action.

Shared values

In any transition period it is particularly important that people manage change in a fashion which echoes the organization's stated values. Successful organizations develop a set of values which underpin the way its employees go about doing business and interacting with each other and which are in line with the strategic objectives of the organization.

Often the development of a customer-focused strategy brings with it a need for greater openness, feedback and teamwork amongst employees. However, the values an organization espouses may turn out to be difficult to uphold in practice. Many companies who try to initiate change via the adoption of value-based programmes end up with superficial results at best and at worst an increase in cynicism and disenchantment among their employees.

One company who used a values-based programme to help them through a difficult period of transition is the international software business SCO. In 1992/93 important challenges faced the company. Competition was fierce and in mid-1993 the company became a publicly quoted operation, which forced on the company additional pressures.

The issue was how the company could grow into the first league and still retain the unique strengths which it had developed in its formative years. These were seen to be characterized by informality, entrepreneurialism, high personal discretion and involvement, scope for personal initiative and open communication. It was felt that the ethos of task-centred individualism was being lost in the transition period. The organization set out to identify managerial values and practices which were essential for the company's continued success and to identify areas for changes in the behaviour of managers and employees.

It ran a series of workshops for all members of the management team where a three-step process was initiated, first to gain an understanding of current values and, second, to define the desired values and then to address the gap.

The workshops were so successful that they were cascaded throughout the organization with team managers facilitating the process among their staff. One of the most powerful outcomes of the process was the realization that employees at all levels had a choice either to control the organization they worked for and to make it a place where they could feel comfortable and motivated, or to be controlled by their organization and to be victims of processes beyond their control. This acted as a very powerful stimulus for action.[11]

Staff

Task groups responsible for the implementation of process improvements, redesigns or reengineering need to consider not only what staff should be involved in the process but also what impact the new ways of working will have on people throughout the organization. The implications may be far reaching. They may include, for example:

- devising new ways of organizing work;
- redesigning jobs;
- coaching and counselling people so they gain an understanding of their new roles;

- designing performance management systems;
- developing individual and team-based rewards;
- designing internal communication mechanisms;
- Extending employees' knowledge base.

Skills

Many changes in processes also involve changes in the skill and knowledge base of the people involved in the process. Task groups who are responsible for implementing the changes need to consider carefully what skill sets need to change to effect the new process and how these skills are best imparted.

People have immense abilities when they are fully trained and focused on key objectives. Telecommunications company Bell Atlantic in the US reduced the time it took to install a high-speed digital link from 30 to three days by drawing on the knowledge and skills of its workers. It provided a tailored training and development programme to all employees involved in the change.

Systems

Task groups need to identify the changes that can be brought about by information technology to help facilitate the new process. This is often an area most associated with business process reengineering when new technology can help fashion new ways of working.

Direct Line, the insurance subsidiary of the Royal Bank of Scotland, has invented an entirely new way of doing business with its customers. The company produced record earnings in 1993 and Peter Wood, who heads the organization, became Britain's highest-paid executive. Information technology played a major part in enabling the company to offer the service without paperwork, front office or layers of management. It provided the tool for developing a business from a 'blank piece of paper' into reality.

One of the considerations the task group will need to make is what are the potential gains which can be reaped from new technology against the potential high cost involved. In a survey carried out by Pearson and Skinner in 1993 many financial service organizations who had undertaken process improvement reviews had not been able to benefit fully from these improvements owing to the lack of investment in technology. Sixty-five per cent of companies interviewed who had adopted process thinking were not prepared to change their existing information technology in spite of recommendations from process review teams. This was because of the large-scale investment which had to be made in existing technology.

 ## How changes will be implemented

A theme repeated throughout this book is that how change is managed is critical to the effective implementation of process thinking.

In a survey of 400 managers carried out by Ashridge Management College, entitled the 1994/95 Ashridge Management Index, nearly half of those questioned were concerned about the impact of change. Over 25 per cent of managers were concerned about issues of organizational change and the difficulties of introducing new ways of working. Twenty-three per cent saw the changing nature of the managerial role as their biggest challenge.

There are several techniques which task groups can use to identify potential barriers to changes and how these can be overcome. A simple technique is force field analysis. This sets out on one side of a piece of paper the driving forces for change and, on the other, the driving forces against change. Figure 9.6 is an example.

Once the force field has been completed, the task group can develop a strategy for minimizing the resistance to change and building on the driving forces for change.

Another tool is the actors/issues matrix. This is a tool which can be used to identify who the key players are in the implementation of the change journey and what issues they are likely to raise. Figure 9.7 is an example produced by type of employee. By anticipating the differing concerns of the different actors within the change scenario, the task groups can clarify objectives for addressing these issues.

The implementation teams will find it beneficial to identify champions for the change process at all levels throughout the

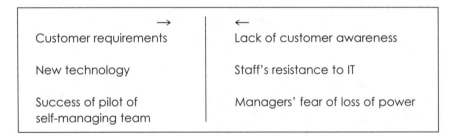

→	←
Customer requirements	Lack of customer awareness
New technology	Staff's resistance to IT
Success of pilot of self-managing team	Managers' fear of loss of power

Figure 9.6 Example of a part-completed force field analysis

organizations. These are people who can exert influence on others to change and who are prepared to change themselves.

The need for individual change was a learning point that emerged from a change programme developed by the pharmaceuticals company, SmithKline Beecham. The company was formed from the merger in 1989 of the US SmithKline Beckman Corporation and British-owned Beecham Group plc. To unite the two companies under one vision statement, a cultural change programme called 'Simply Better' was developed. Its aim was to create one corporate culture taking the best from both companies and providing a common way of working. A training and education programme was developed which set out to define roles clearly, devolve decision making and provide employees with practical methods and tools for defining core processes and making improvements.

One of the key learning-points from the programme was that the process owner population, middle managers, needed to be actively involved and consider themselves part of the programme to make it work. They had to change to help others change.

Overcoming resistance to change

Task groups can adopt many routes to overcome resistance to change. These include:
- explanation of the need to change;
- persuading people that change will happen and is necessary;
- involving people in creating the change;
- bringing about realization that the organization is committed to change;

The board of a business is likely to be won over by the benefits

Actor	Executives	Middle managers	Workforce
Issue			
Time commitment	X	X	
Resource challenge	X	X	
Downsizing		X	X
Communication		X	X

Figure 9.7 Example of an actor/issue matrix

that will derive from a change programme in terms of profit generation or cost saving or improved performance, etc. There is also a requirement to convince senior managers that changes will result in more effective working. Managers also need to be made aware of change requirements relative to the external market and for staff it is all of these dimensions plus the potential benefits to customers which the changes can bring. Everyone needs to know how the changes will affect them.

Financial services group Clerical Medical Investment has done much to actively involve its staff in change. Clerical Medical began a total quality management programme in the 1990s in response to the need to improve and tightly control costs while improving quality. Two years down the line it recognized the programme had reached a plateau. Initial enthusiasm for the initiative was waning; improvements had been made but they needed to be sustained.

The society decided that process management was the route forward. They recognized that in the past management had ignored the importance of processes. As a result, activities had become broken down into small tasks, staff had lost sight of the whole task and with it the customer. As many people were involved in the service chain, each step in the chain provided opportunity for loss, error and bottlenecks.

The society decided to train its people in how to unravel the processes, develop their own measures, implement controls and then put in place workflow management tools themselves. Courses were held for managers and staff in techniques such as:

– work measurement;
– statistical process control;
– process improvement;
– product planning.

During the training all staff commented on the waste involved in compiling statistics and measures which were never used or seen again. As a result a process measurement system was installed in all business units in the Bristol head office. Called 'Performance Management', the aim was to achieve measurement that impacted on the future and was not focused on the past.

The programme was piloted in two areas using techniques such as activity sampling, diary sheets analysis and process management. In one area several other attempts had been made to identify the root cause of the lengthy turnaround times and delays in service which had resulted in declining service standards. When 'Performance Management' began supervisors and staff were very involved in setting up the scheme and following it through. They spent two weeks collecting data, another two analysing work activity and within six weeks productivity and customer service levels had risen dramatically. Staff were better motivated and turnaround times were reduced.

As a result of the pilot, process management is being rolled out to the rest of the business units in a three-month programme. The approach taken for the roll-out is again one of staff owner-ship of the initiative. This is seen as pivotal to its success.[12]

Piloting improvements

As the Clerical Medical example demonstrates, one means of minimizing the impact of organizational change is to pilot the changes before they are rolled out in other parts of the organization. There are advantages and disadvantages to this approach. The disadvantages are that the proposed changes will take longer to implement if they are piloted initially. The major advantage is that, where the pilot is successful, it demonstrates to other parts of the organization or work areas that the new process brings about improvements.

One organization who has successfully used a pilot to demonstrate the power of process thinking is Surrey Police. Currently police forces in the UK are under immense pressure to improve their performance to the customer. Surrey Police's first service charter was developed in 1992. Like other police forces, Surrey Police have evolved piecemeal since the last century and has been traditionally modelled on military lines, with separate functional divisions specializing in, among other things, traffic, community relations, criminal investigations, training and uniform operations.

Surrey Police have adopted a process thinking approach to ensure its service quality using the notion of added value to its customers. It set up a pilot study in the area of burglary investigations with a view to designing or redesigning its core processes in order to improve the number of detected burglaries, thereby improving customer and officer satisfaction. As a result of the pilot study a new process has been developed. The underlying concept is to obtain the best possible evidence-supported linkages among sets of burglaries. This has been implemented by the first-on-a-scene, one-stop burglary team who plan and deliver a well co-ordinated service.

The pilot scheme has set the way for other core processes to be redesigned. This has helped Surrey Police cope with improving its service delivery and organizational structure in an environment where increasing demands and resources are combined with growing financial pressures.

Communicating change

The way change is communicated is vital. The worst mechanism is to allow changes to be communicated via the grapevine. Change is best communicated on a face-to-face basis. Where a large number of people are involved in change this may not always be possible, although large events can be held to explain initially the reasons for the change and what the impact will be. But large-scale announcements are not enough. People should always be given an opportunity to discuss the changes on a one-to-one basis.

Sometimes it proves beneficial to fashion a new way of describing the changes which will take place by creating a common language for change. At the National & Provincial Building Society a major change programme, started in 1990, set out to build an organization which operated as a 'team of teams', serving the customer. A completely new way of doing business was established, led by a group of senior managers, called the Direction Management Team who gave clarity of purpose to the change programme.

To help break away from the old way of thinking a new internal language was created to describe the transformed organization. For example, the departments became 'team' and managers, 'team leaders'. Jobs were called 'roles' and staff renamed 'players'.

What individuals are interested in is how the changes will affect them. Team briefing, newsletters and meetings provide useful vehicles which can be used both to disseminate information and to gain feedback.

When Whitbread Beer Company began planning the changes which would be brought about by its business reengineering programme, the potential impact on people was a key consideration. The project team recognized that an exercise of this nature was bound to create uncertainty and would inevitably impact on the company's organization and ultimately jobs. Other aspects of the people impact were anticipated by a review of reward and recognition arrangements to ensure that they supported the kind of behaviour which would make the programme succeed.

Keeping people informed was another planning consideration although it proved to be difficult. Positioning the study prior to commencement was not easy because it was difficult for staff to envisage how it would work and it created a fear that major change would result. Although there were regular updates during the various phases, the messages were difficult to convey as people were most concerned about anything that might impact on them personally and this could only really emerge during the implementation phase.

The planning phase had anticipated a need to help people through the change process and a change management programme was developed using external consultants. This resulted in the development of a 'Changing Gear' workshop which allowed people going through change to assess and understand the impact of change on themselves and to plan to implement the change most effectively. Whitbread Beer Company intend that all personnel will attend a workshop as change is supplemented over the next two years.

Various means were used to overcome resistance to change starting with involving as many people as possible in the teams working on the business reengineering activities. This has been particularly extended into the implementation process where staff consultation has been attempted as far as possible. As much information as can be allowed is being made available to generate an atmosphere of openness and honesty – part of the company's key business values.

An increasing use of feedback mechanisms is also being attempted. In the past there has been criticism of being talked at (not to), with little opportunity for comment. To monitor the reaction to the change process an existing staff attitude survey was adapted to measure key facts. Whitbread Beer Company's Quality of Worklife survey is carried out every six months and enables trends to be monitored.[13]

Training and education

Training and education should play a large part in the change process. The emphasis should be on supporting the change process with relevant training.

Quite often when changes occur the emphasis is on training front-line support staff who will be involved in the process. However, managers also need help in understanding the behaviours that are required of them as part of the new way of working.

In preparation for change, it often helps to cascade a programme of education beginning with the senior management team. As employees need an opportunity to voice their concerns and to question the impact of the changes, education and training are best undertaken in a participative fashion. There is an increasing trend towards a workshop style of training. Anglia Water, for example, held a series of workshops to herald the changes that were to take place as a result of process thinking. These were led by members of senior management.

The commitment to training requires more than just money. It also requires time and the willingness to release people at the right time. Of course not everyone can be trained to take on new ways of working. While every effort should be made to allow time, it may not be possible for some people to take on new skills, and

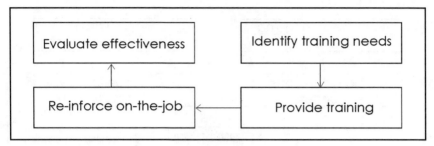

Figure 9.8 The training and development cycle

redeployment and ultimately severance has to be considered as a last course.

Training should be seen as part of an ongoing development cycle. In addition to skills training in new processes and technology, behavioural training may be required to facilitate the change. Typical areas of need when process improvements take place include :
— educating managers in their role as coach;
— effective team building;
— customer handling skills;
— information technology skills.
It is important that after training has taken place, it is re-enforced in the workplace and constantly renewed and updated.

Figure 9.8 shows the training and development cycle.

 ## Monitoring the change process

During the transition phase, task groups should ensure that the people who are responsible for implementing the change plans agree a clearly defined goal, broken down into specific tasks with clear timings and responsibilities.

The task groups should also consider what mechanisms they can put in place for measuring the performance against the goals set so that successes can be evaluated. One way of achieving this is to set objectives and standards of each phase of the change programme and to establish critical areas of performance. Measures need to be developed for which data can be obtained with ease and which are closely related to the changes being

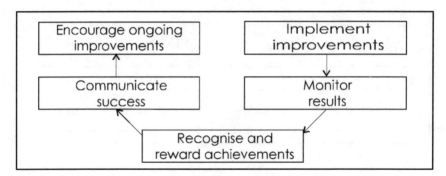

Figure 9.9 The improvement cycle

implemented. As external events over which the process participants have no control can effect performance, these should be recorded.

As it is sometimes difficult to identify performance indicators it is useful at this stage to look back on the assessments which were undertaken as part of the detailed analysis phase to ascertain which measures would still be meaningful given the improvements to the process.

The most important arbitrator of improved performance should be the customer. Task groups should monitor customers' reaction to change and continue to improve in response to customer feedback.

 Celebrate success

Behind every successful process are successful people. As the Whitbread Beer Company example given earlier in the chapter demonstrates, often reward and recognition schemes need to be revamped to complement the new way of working.

Once the improvement is in place and the organization is reaping its benefits, it is motivated to celebrate its success. This can be achieved by team events, individual recognition or company-wide conferences where the organization can look at what has been achieved and recognize that continued success involves ongoing improvements.

Figure 9.9 illustrates the improvement cycle.

■ Summary

- This chapter deals with evaluating potential solutions, making recommendations and implementing improvements.
- It outlines four techniques which can be adopted to evaluate solutions: three-star rating, scenario analysis, cost–benefit analysis and strategic fit/customer needs analysis.
- After discussing what to include in a presentation to senior management on the review, an outline of project management tools which can be used in the implementation process is discussed. These include action plans and milestone charts.
- A variety of methods for implementing effective change programmes is outlined including the use of force field analysis, the actor/issue matrix and McKinsey's seven S's framework.
- The piloting of improvements is discussed, together with the need to communicate change, provide education and training, monitor improvements and communicate success.

CHAPTER

10

PROCESS IMPROVEMENT IN ACTION

The preceding chapters have discussed process thinking as a tool for change, methodologies for undertaking a process review and how to go about implementing improvements to processes and manage change effectively.

This chapter reiterates the learning points from the book through case studies of three organizations who have adopted process thinking to bring about improvements in their performance. The organizations have been chosen for their differing size and scope to demonstrate that process thinking can be used as a tool for change in a variety of industry sectors.

 Barr and Stroud

In 1987 Barr and Stroud, an historic Glasgow engineering firm that had been sole supplier of periscopes to the Royal Navy since 1916 and whose work in optronics was 96 per cent defence-related, turned in record profits of £8.6 million on sales of £85.3 million. Three years later, in 1990, the Berlin Wall had been breached, defence contracts for submarines, missiles and tanks were melting away with the end of the Cold War, and Barr and Stroud was peering over the edge of a cliff with losses of £4.4 million.

'We realized we had better change, and change quickly,' says Tom O'Neill, the tough Glaswegian managing director brought in by parent company Pilkington Optronics to stop the rot. The company should have gone for radical change in 1985, says

O'Neill, but its management then thought it would have time to do it gradually. As it was, 'We knew that if we didn't get it right it would be the end of the road for the whole company,' says O'Neill.

Two years on, Barr and Stroud was in the black again with profits of £1 million in 1991/92. It had abandoned its sprawling Edwardian plant in Glasgow's Anniesland district and had taken an astounding £15 million out of stock and inventory costs. A mere 10 per cent success in meeting contracted delivery dates had leapt to 90 per cent (still improving), lead times had halved from 15 to seven months, productivity had risen by 30 per cent and sales per employee increased from £25,000 to £60,000.

The workforce had also been slashed from over 2,000 to around 800, at compensation costs of £10,000–£12,000 a head. Overall costs, however, were down by £7 million a year and the company has launched a new non-defence product, a thermal imager that can 'see' ten kilometres in the dark. Orders totalled £1 million before production started.

The Glasgow company had tinkered with change under its old management, looking at an IT solution and calling in Andersen Consulting, which had evolved a software program designed for the aerospace and defence industries. But the newly appointed MD O'Neill, and operations director Lawrie Rumens, brought in at the same time, realized that it was essentially a problem of business strategy that could not be solved by IT alone.

Andersen now switched to the reengineering track and, says partner Mike Ward, enabled the company to work out its redesign internally. A basic starting point was the Three-Two-One system, deciding the core competencies that only the Glasgow plant could perform and pushing out two other successive circles of manufacturing – modules and components – to plants in Wales. This enabled the company to quit its rambling Anniesland plant and move to the smaller, more compactly planned factory at Linthouse.

The factory, shaped like a submarine with a tall 'conning tower' that serves an essential function – the 60-foot-long periscopes have to be tested vertically – is completely open plan, which contributes to a simple workflow pattern as well as instilling the new 'single status' image of the company. There is now one dining room for everybody in place of six graded ones;

no offices for anyone; one car park and a similar benefits package for all employees.

Further analysis of the company's functional structure revealed a highly people-intensive business, with 210 working in materials planning, 70 in finance and 65 in administration, for example. There was inadequate management information and, despite the presence of 60 'expediters' chasing work in progress round the factory, only 10 per cent of contracts were being delivered on time. 'We were up to two years late on some orders,' recalls O'Neill.

Management layers were reduced from nine to four throughout the company – in some areas to just three. 'Middle management was taken completely out of its comfort zones', says O'Neill. The comfort zones had included offices, and a number did not take kindly to the new exposed style of management. O'Neill told them briskly that if he and Lawrie Rumens could do it, 'so can you'. Operations director Rumens has his desk on the shopfloor, Japanese-style.

Essential to the change of culture was the establishment of multi-disciplinary teams comprising directors, managers, engineers and operators working together on the shopfloor. 'People who are now in teams have a different view of their functions,' says Rumens. 'It's a great sharpening of what jobs are about.'

The existence of teams, interacting quickly and informally, stripped time and waste out of the system. Engineering changes that used to take three and a half months with memos being exchanged through internal mail now happen 'in minutes' because one man simply goes over to talk to another at a nearby desk.

'You need change agents at every level, not just at the top,' says Rumens. But Andersen's partner Ward pinpoints the attitude of the MD and operations director as the driving force. 'It was their visibility and involvement,' he says. 'It's the difference between a CEO who is merely willing to sign a consultant's cheque and one who lets his managers know: "I believe in this and I'm going to hold you accountable".'

Figure 10.1 shows the old and the new structure at Barr and Stroud.

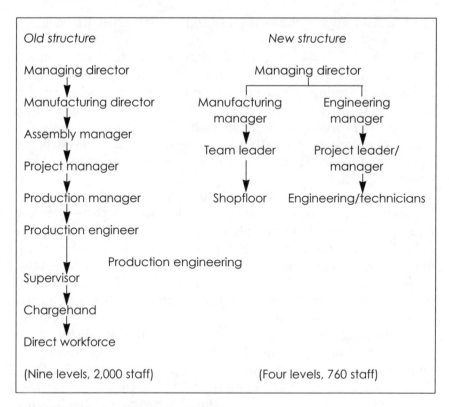

Figure 10.1 Barr and Stroud's old and new structure[14]

 British Alcan Aluminium

A 'patchwork quilt' approach to BPR has been adopted by British Alcan Aluminium. In three years it has completed some modest but effective projects. The company's experience has been so successful that it has become a paradigm for other manufacturing companies with reengineering dilemmas. It has developed a novel way to train managers in BPR techniques and identified four preconditions necessary to make reengineering successful.

British Alcan's move into reengineering started in response to the need to improve efficiency and deliver better customer service. The organization's link with Nippon Light Metal – its Japanese sister company in which Alcan has a 49 per cent stake has proved especially beneficial. In fact, Jon Woolven, a business analyst at British Alcan, says the company's approach to BPR grew out of kaizen, the continuous improvement methodology perfected in Japan, but it differs in that it aims for step-change rather than incremental performance improvements.

Woolven says that Alcan's approach to BPR is tailored to suit its own culture. 'We stress the value of participation, rigorous analysis of data, visual displays of problems and performance and the documentation of agreed procedures. We believe in looking outwards focusing improvements on the customer.'

In a typical Alcan BPR project there are four phases – preparation, classroom training, analysis and design, and reorganization.

Preparation lasts about a month, during which managers focus on understanding the problem and exploring options. They collect data, choose a project team and define the target. Says Woolven: 'That really is the make or break stage. It is crucial to get all of that right.'

Next comes classroom training based on a computerized simulation exercise. Managers reengineer an imaginary quotation process encountering the kind of problems they will meet in a real-life project. 'The exercise,' says Woolven, 'shows the team that it is possible to make startling improvements in a business process. That is a good lesson before they meet the real world, because they are often very sceptical of their ability to do that.'

The analysis and design phase takes about five days. The BPR team works with a facilitator or coach to redesign the process and document the new procedures that will apply. With that successfully completed, the team starts the implementation phase, usually taking about a month. An example from British Alcan's patchwork quilt shows how this approach works in practice.

A small British Alcan company which assembles luggage racks and light fittings was half-way through a contract. It was falling behind schedule and, says Woolven, 'on-time delivery was awful. The customer was for ever calling up and changing its mind about the sequence of deliveries, but since the production lead time was three weeks, the company could never respond in time. The shop floor was piled high with inventory.' And, ominously, the contract was due for renewal.

Using the four-stage BPR approach, a team devised a five-point solution. This involved re-laying the plant, making a small product redesign, multi-skilling the fabricators to form a production cell, discarding redundant stock and introducing a kanban scheduling system.

As a result, the company was able to hold a stock of components which it could assemble to order in two days. Says Woolven: 'Within three months the company was ahead of schedule with virtually 100 per cent of on-time delivery.' Inventory was reduced. Most important, the contract was renewed and the company also won a contract for a different product.

Woolven warns there are a few preconditions if a company is to reap the benefit from this approach. 'First and foremost, the business must be well managed with good open communications to explain the reasons for change.'

A second precondition is to make BPR part of a strategic plan. Too many companies like the sound of BPR but have no idea of how to apply it in their own organization. Says Woolven: 'It shouldn't work that way round. You have got to see how BPR can serve your strategic need.'

The third precondition is backing from top managers. 'Managers must demonstrate their commitment up front to follow through with the changes,' says Woolven.

The final point is where the hard decision comes. Many BPR projects aim to reduce the headcount in organizations. Woolven says this should not be part of the responsibility of the BPR team. 'We had one example in our company where we attempted that and it set peer against peer. We are still trying to recover from the morale problems which came from that.'

Cutting staff is a management responsibility, suggests Woolven. 'They have to grasp that message and they can't delegate it to the rest of the organization.'[15]

 ## Santa Cruz Operation (SCO)

Founded in 1979, the Santa Cruz Operation, SCO, is an open systems software supplier which opened its European headquarters in the UK at the end of 1986. From its technically pioneering beginnings it is now a leading open systems software developer and supplier for those computers which are based on Intel microprocessors (the largest part of the personal computer market) a market which it helped to create.

While the company has grown in Europe from 50 to over 400 people in 1994 with a turnover of £60 million, by 1991 it felt an compelling need to review the way it served the customer. Potentially service was identified as a key differentiator in an increasingly competitive market. It was important to the company's continuing growth and success that service levels were consistently superior to its competitors.

The company offers a technical telephone and E-mail support helpline for its customers. As business demands grew dramatically, customers were increasing and the backlog of calls requiring attention was spiralling. The first response was to recruit extra staff and install a new computer system to log and distribute the calls. But new technology did not change things as much as management hoped. Improved technical training followed but there was still scope for improvement.

Staff were under pressure. The company was putting in a lot of effort to run to stand still, trying to fix piecemeal issues which the staff did not always seem fully behind. To get to the root of the problem, it was agreed that a review should be taken of the total business. Further discussion led to a customer focus programme of quality improvement.

The Managing Director launched the programme which started with a two-day workshop which all customer-focusing managers and staff attended. It involved everyone in considering: What was the mission of the company and their departments? What were the key problem areas? The programme was initiated by the Customer Services Department and followed by other departments. Each group had a say in defining the mission of their department. This was consolidated into the service mission.

Managers had felt that the culture must move forward – some employees had an altogether inward 'tetchy' feel which could be misinterpreted as arrogance. Notes from a management brainstorm at the time reflect these culture change issues:

Culture now	*Future*
Technically orientated	Service oriented
Sometimes little 'ownership'	Readily owns problems

Many problems passed to managers	
Individuals work in isolation	Teamwork and co-operation
Few ideas acted upon	Continuous improvement

To support this change in culture managers identified a number of improvement areas. They recognized that employee involvement was a key aspect of the whole scheme. As management's confidence in this process of empowerment grew, so employees were entrusted with more.

The programme started off with little consultation. A few employees had to be cajoled to attend the workshops but soon more people were taking an interest: they had a better chance to contribute outside their technical specialism. Managers were surprised and encouraged by the suggestions for improvement. In the early years the company had grown at speed with some systems and procedures which had now outlived their effectiveness. In the workshops, small groups worked on typical customer requirements which were the key problems. Where were the bottlenecks? How long did calls take to get processed from start to finish? Each group presented to the rest of the workshop who were then asked to review what could be done to improve matters (see Figure 10.2).

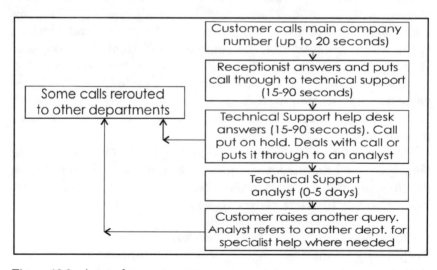

Figure 10.2   A sample process map

The next stage was to set up a process improvement team of six volunteers to work on the action points from the workshops. In the first three months 25 improvements were suggested, some big some small. Staff interest and involvement became higher. The way customer issues were handled became a regular talking-point in a new way.

Some early cynicism and resistance were overcome by patient management who were prepared to listen and respond to difficulties and praise improvements. But success through involvement started to breed success, and positive feedback was given. Greater staff autonomy became possible. Customers were invited along to make suggestions, at the instigation of employees.

Out of the workshops one problem emerged regularly – at times customer calls were being routed around the company to different departments with no one talking ownership for the issue and sometimes staff unsure who dealt with what issue. This was leading to customer frustration and even occasionally to calls being lost en route.

The process improvement team set to work on this issue and representatives of interested functions contributed ways to resolve it. The outcome was the circulation of an information sheet setting out where to refer particular queries – product information to sales, press enquiries to PR, training courses to training and so on. Further training was given to key staff, using flowcharts as check-lists.

At the start of programmes some managers had set rather conservative improvement objectives but as the programme got underway everyone began to realize the scope and possibilities of the programme. The turning-point was when the momentum of the staff built up to the extent that they wanted to explore and make more suggestions to resolve many more issues than a simple customer service improvement programme.

Critically customer measures were put in place to assess improvements. Customer surveys were started and continued every six months. The survey questions covered such areas as usefulness of information, problem solving, courteousness and professionalism of service. Performance standards were initiated for each level of staff and individual and team performance regularly reviewed covering availability on-call, maintaining database information, times to answer queries.

Customer satisfaction began to improve and not just through survey measures, which in themselves showed impressive sustained improvements. Gradually letters of praise started to appear. Measurement through the call backlog and the customer surveys showed a marked improvement which had continued.

During the changes it was felt more regular information needed to be given to all employees, so monthly team briefing was introduced. It covered not just company progress but regular customer information and industry news.

Training and development have always been seen as integral to the success of the programme. Skills development through the two-day workshops was supplemented by the team leaders coaching their staff. The improvement process team was trained in process improvement techniques, group problem solving and discussion leading. Managers were given the same training as staff and also coaching skills.

Many of the employees are young and eager to acquire new knowledge and skills which will enhance their career development. The programme gave a powerful means to encourage and achieve this energy.

After the workshops, the next stage was to establish working groups with all departments to improve the service each was offering. Joint task groups were set up. These groups helped foster the culture of the internal customer. For example, following a customer service workshop the order processing team identified the distributor shipping department as an area to improve. Too frequently paperwork went astray or was not processed correctly. Geographical distance added to misunderstandings. The order processing team sat down with distribution shipping and went through the issues and processes. They exchanged information where necessary and jointly revised processes. Co-operation, coaching and working jointly produced noticeable improvements. Over the last year this has been developed much further with a total review of the distribution and sales procedures as part of gaining ISO 9001.

Formal quarterly reviews were built into the process at which the results of customer surveys are also analysed. Internal departments have been encouraged to carry out surveys on their internal customers.

Three years later, profitability and revenue per employee have shown encouraging signs of improvement to reaching record levels. As a result of better processes more is being achieved without proportionately increasing staff. The culture has shifted to a more customer-orientated approach and a more involving one. Managers are now seriously considering moving a step further in personal and team accountability by introducing self-managing work teams. The SCO approach to process thinking provides a straightforward and participative method of making it easier for customers to do business with an organization.[16]

 ## Conclusions

The interest in and importance given to business reengineering is clearly justified in the business performance arena, with its emphasis on examining inter-related activities within an organization.

Although this method can bring about dramatic improvements, it must be set in its appropriate context: as a tool for change.

Attention must be paid in particular to changing the culture of a company, the bedrock of its values and beliefs. This can be a long-term and sometimes painful process which needs careful and active management.

Process improvements should be reviewed and renewed just as employee attitudes and skills should be constantly addressed if an organization is truly to achieve quantum leaps in performance.

CHAPTER

11

SOURCES OF INFORMATION

 Books

Baden-Fuller, C. and Stopford, J. (1992), *Rejuvenating the Mature Corporation*, London: Routledge Books.

BPR in the Public Sector – An Overview of Business Process Re-engineering (1994), London: HMSO Publications.

Coulson Thomas C. *et al.* (1994), *BPR: Myth and Reality*, London: Kogan Page.

Davenport, T. (1993), *Process Innovation*, Boston: Harvard Business School Press.

Goldratt, E. and Cox, J. (1984), *The Goal*, Aldershot: Gower.

Hamel, G. and Prahalad, C. (1994), *Competing for the Future*, HBR Press.

Hammer, M. and Champy, J. (1993), *Re-engineering the Corporation*, London: Nicholas Brealey Publishing.

Kay, J. (1993), *Foundations of Corporate Success*, Oxford: Oxford University Press.

Obolensky, N. (1994), *Practical business reengineering*, London: Kogan Page.

Peters, T. (1992), *Liberation Management*, New York: Alfred A. Knopf.

Schwartz, P. (1991), *The Art of the Long View* (1991), London: Century Business.

Scott-Morton, M. (ed) (1991), *The Corporation of the 1990s,* Oxford: Oxford University Press.

Semler, R. (1993), *Maverick*, London: Century Business Press.

Senge, P. et al. (1994), *The Fifth Discipline Fieldbook*, London: Nicholas Brealey Publishing.

Towers, S. (1994), *Business Process Reengineering*, Cheltenham: Stanley Thorn.

Waterman, R. (1994), *The Frontiers of Excellence*, London: Nicholas Brealey Publishing.

 Journal

Process Product Watch. Quarterly review of reengineering and process management products produced by Enix Ltd, tel: 0181 332 0210

 Organizations

Strategic Planning Society
Re-engineering and Radical Change Group
17 Portland Place
London W1N 3AF
Tel : 0171 636 7737

Institute of Business Process Reengineering
1 Cecil Court

London Road
Enfield
Middlesex EN2 3AF
Tel: 0181-366 6718

Business Intelligence
Forum House
1 Graham Road
London SW19 3SW
Tel: 0181 544 1830

Organizes seminars and conferences on Business Process
Re-engineering

Cambridge Market Intelligence
London House
Parkgate Road
London SW11 4NQ
Tel: 0171 924 7117

Produces reports on aspects of Business Processes.

REFERENCES

1. Cobra report available from Adaptation Ltd. Fax: 0181 857 5947.
2. *Financial Times* article written by Tim Dickson, 5.2.95. 'Executive Heal Thyself'.
3. *Mail on Sunday* article written by Paul Eastham, 9.2.94. 'Story of Waste'.
4. Based on article by Carol Kennedy and Stuart Rock in *Director*, August 1993, 'If we didn't get it right it would be the end of the road for the company'.
5. Based on article by Carol Kennedy and Stuart Rock in *Director*, August 1993, 'If we didn't get it right it would be the end of the road for the company'.
6. *Re-engineering – the critical success factors*, report published by British Intelligence, 1994.
7. Reproduced with kind permission of Chris Hughes, ICL.
8. Based on article by Carol Kennedy and Stuart Rock in *Director*, August 1993, 'If we didn't get it right it would be the end of the road for the company'.
9. *Management Training*, February 1995 article 'Water Margins' by Jane Bird.
10. Reproduced by kind permission of Tim Williams, The Whitbread Beer Company.
11. Reproduced with kind permission of Steve Macaulay, SCO Ltd.
12. Based on an article by Elizabeth Gooch and Geoff Wilmer, 'Where to After BPR?' *Management Services*, September 1994.
13. Reproduced by kind permission of Tim Williams, The

Whitbread Beer Company.

14. Based on article by Carol Kennedy and Stuart Rock in *Director*, August 1993, 'If we didn't get it right it would be the end of the road for the company'.

15. Based on article by Peter Bartram in *Management Today*, July 1994, 'Re-engineering Revised'.

16. Based on article by Steve Macaulay and Sarah Cook, published in The Journal of Corporate Transformation, Spring 1994, Volume 1, No. 4 and reproduced by kind permission of John Wiley & Sons.

INDEX